CROCHET
FOR
BEGINNERS

LEARN STEP BY STEP CROCHETING WITH PICTURE ILLUSTRATIONS, CROCHET PATTERNS AND STITCHES

(QUICK AND EASY GUIDE).

BY

MAMO

Contents

DISCLAIMER

Even though the author and the publisher worked together to verify that the material contained in this book was accurate at the time of publication.

The author and the publisher shall not be liable to any party for any damage, damage, or destruction caused by errors, omissions, inaccuracies, negligence, accident, or any other cause.

Thanks for choosing this book, I would really like to hear your opinion, please consider giving us a honest rewiev on Amazon.

Introduction to Crochet

What Is Crochet?

Crochet is an embroidery method that utilizes a crochet hook with fiber or similar material. This fiber is most usually wool or crochet thread, but it could also be leather, rope, twine, or other inventive content.

Crochet fans are looking forward to finishing crochet creations that are usually useful, desirable, or helpful items in some way. Common initiatives typically involve Afghans, crocheted blankets, baby booties, sweaters, beanies, and squares of granny, shawls, pouches, tote bags, and many others. A number of different things can be crocheted, including brooches, socks, and curtains.

It is also important to use different components in other products to crochet. Crochet trims as well as edgings, for example, are common projects; you may add them to crocheted products, knitted items, as well as sewn pieces (including ready-made shop-bought items), such as purchasing some shoes, towels, and/or pillow cases, and applying a crocheted finish to each.

Crochet History

The term crochet is taken from the Medieval French word croc or croche, which means cord. Crocheting, that means hook basically.

As it was called in English, French, Belgians, Italians, as well as Spanish-speaking individuals, do call crochet. The skill is recognised in Holland as haken, in Denmark haekling, in Norway hekling, and also in Sweden virkning.

Due to archeological finds, historical documents, and artistic renderings of various kinds, certain types of handwork-knitting, lace, and weaving-can be dated well back into time. But whenever and wherever crochet rose to prominence, nobody's really sure.

The phrase comes from croc, or croche, a word for hook in Middle French, and also the word for hook in Old Norse is krokr.

"The modem practice of true crochet as known today was created during the 16th century," says American crochet pioneer and world traveler Annie Potter. "It became popular as' crochet lace' in France and' thread lace' in England."

As well as, she tells us, in 1916, Walter Edmund Roth met ancestors of Guyana Indians then discovered traces of true crochet.

A further writer / researcher, Denmark's Lis Paludan, who restricted her quest for Europe's crochet roots, placed forth 3 interesting thoughts. One: Crochet developed in Arabia, spread east to Tibet and west to Spain, from where it migrated to other Countries on the Arabian trading routes.

Two: Crochet's earliest records originated from South America, where someone said that a native group used crochet decorations in puberty rituals. Three: Early reports of three-dimensional dolls employed in crochet were documented in China.

Yet, says Paludan, the truth of the matter is that there is "no compelling evidence as to how ancient crochet practice might be or where it originated from. Until 1800, it was difficult to find traces of crochet in Europe. Some sources say that crochet was regarded as' nun's job' or' nun's lace' in Italy as far away as the 1500s, where it was employed by nuns for religious textiles,"s.

Her research has given rise to examples of lace creating some kind of lace tape, most of which have been maintained, but "all indications are that crochet has not been recognised in Italy quite far back as 16th century"-but under no name.

Studies shows that crochet was actually more specifically derived from Chinese needlework, a very ancient form of embroidery found in Turkey, India, Persia, and North Africa that entered Europe in the 1700s and was referred to as "tambouring," from those in the French "tambour" or drum. A backdrop cloth is placed on a plate in this technique.

Under the cloth is kept the working yarn. A needle with a hook is inserted downwards, and through the fabric, a loop of the working thread is drawn. The hook is then inserted a little further along with the loop still on the hook, and then another loop of that same working thread is taken up and waited to form a chain stitch thru the first loop.

The hooks of the tambour were as thin as needles of sewing, so the work had to be done with really fine thread.

Tambour developed in to what the French termed "crochet in the air" at the end of the 18th century when the fabric of the background was discarded, and the stitch worked alone.

In the early 1800s, crochet started to appear by Europe and was offered a massive boost by Mlle. Riego de la Branchardiere, who has been best remembered for her ability to make crochet variations that could readily be duplicated by taking old-style needle as well as bobbin lace styles.

She authored many trend books in order to start copying her designs by millions of women. Miss. Riego also helped popularize "lace-like" crochet, also named Irish crochet. Irish crochet was a practical lifesaver for the citizens of Ireland.

This lifted them off of their potato famine, which persisted from 1845 to 1850 and plunged them into abject poverty. In those days, comfortable living standards for the Irish were severe.

A wide range of fabrics have been used across the ages: feathers, grasses, reeds, horse hair and sinew, corn, flax, leather, gold and silver and copper fibers, silk, woolen thread, wool yarns (soft zephyr yam, luster yarn, double cable yarn, carpet yarn), cotton yarns (anchor and estramadura), silk threads (cordonnet and floss), linen strings, hemp threads, mohair, chenille, modern mixtures, meta combinations.

We now have a huge selection of linen, wool, silk as well as organic yarns at our fingertips. With these uncommon materials such as copper cable, plastic strips, sisal, jute, fabric scraps, unspun wool, and sometimes even dog hair, we could also crochet.

And what about the device for crochet? We are now going into a yarn shop or Costco and purchasing metal, plastic, or steel hooks in over 25 size options.

Though, in ancient times, they used everything they could get their hands on-first fingers, after which hooks made from metal, wood, fishbone, animal bone, horn, old spoons, teeth of thrown away combs, brass, mother-of-pearl, morse, tortoiseshell, ivory, copper, steel, vulcanite, ebonite, silver as well as agate.

In Dublin at the period of the great purge (1845 to 1850), that at least one individual used to make fine Irish crochet was indeed a needle or a steep wire threaded into a cork or slice of timber or tree bark, with both the end filed down and twisted into a tiny loop.

Person-and it was the men's role-created his craftsmanship for practical reasons in the early centuries. To catching animals as well as snare fish or birds, hunters, as well as fishermen, produced knotted chains of twisted fabrics, cords, or strips of fabric. Other implementations included braided game bags, fishing nets as well as kitchen utensils that were open-worked.

To important occasions like those of religious ceremonies, holidays, weddings, or funerals, handwork has been extended to include informal decoration. In crochet-like adornments and ornamental drippings for arms, ankles as well as wrists, most of us see ceremonial outfits.

In Europe of the 16th century, aristocracy and the wealthy were adorned in gold trimmings, gowns, hats, headpieces-and the poor folk would only hope of wearing these items. And, it's thought, crochet was created as the emulation of the lace of the rich man by the poor people.

Continuing into the Victorian era, crochet designs were popular for flowerpot holders, bird cage covers, visiting card frames, lamp mats and shades, wastepaper containers, tablecloths, antimacassars (or "antis," covers to shield chairbacks from hair oil worn by men in the mid-1800s), cigarette packs, purses, men's caps, and waistcoats, even a footwarming rug to be put undead.

People were also busy crocheting Afghans from 1900 to 1930, sleeping rugs, walking rugs, chaise lounge, sleigh rugs, vehicle rugs, cushions, coffee and teapot cozies, and hot water bottle coverings. During this period, potholders rendered their first appearances and then became a standard of the arsenal of that same crocheter.

Then, of course, there is something going on. Crochet started off as an impressionistic medium of communication in the 1960s and 1970s that can now be seen in three-dimensional paintings, textile pieces, or rugs and tapestries portraying abstract and practical patterns and scenes.

Comparing crochet techniques from the past against those we employ today is fascinating. For illustration, it is recorded in the Dutch journal, Penelope, during the period 1824 to 1833 that both the yarn and the hook had to be kept in the hand while holding and the yarn moved from the right forefinger over the hook.

The thread is kept in the right hand as well as the wool in the left in crochet textbooks from the 1840s, as right-handers do now.

In a German publishing dated 1847, it indicated that you should "keep the very same tightness, either crochet crudely or crochet tightly, otherwise you won't achieve an attractive even texture. Moreover, if you don't work on the round, you need to split off your yarn at just the end of each row, as this provides the crocheted item a finer finish." At the flip of the 20th century, this change occurred.

Researcher Lis Paludan theorizes that perhaps the exhortation to retain the same tension "seems to mean that crochet needles are all of the same width and that the crocheter was required to work in the right tension according to fashion."

Ancient design directions, dating back to the mid-1800s, suggested that the hook was only to be used in the second half of the stitch using a single crochet stich.

Jenny Lambert, a German, wrote in 1847 that putting the sole crochet in the back half of that same stitching was useful to make table runners and so on, but running the hook through those loops could be used to "crochet sole for shoes and other things that must be thicker than normal, but the procedure is not ideal for designs."

Another simply copied the work of someone else until ideas were recorded. Specimens were made, sewn and attached like scrapbooks, stitched on large strips of fabric, or left loose in a bag or case. Writer Annie Potter discovered many of these scrapbooks in use by nuns in Spain in her travels, dating back to the late 1800s.

A further way of collecting stitch patterns was to knit various stitches in large, thin bands together-some created by parents, some begun at school then added to it over the years. (Subsequently, in Europe, around 1916 to around 1926, readers were able to buy tiny pattern variations together with their yarn.) In 1824, the first crochet patterns documented to date were printed.

The first designs of color work crochet were for silver and gold silk thread purses.

In many nations, crochet books have been discovered, mostly translated from one language into another. Mlle was perhaps the most popular crochet specialist. Riego de la Branchardiere, who has written over a 100 novels, has released many on crochet.

The crochet publications from the mid-1800s were slim but also included woodcut drawings, only around 4 inches by 6 inches. According to Paludan, these tiny gems included designs for white buttons-like collars, cuffs, lace, insertions including caps for women and kids, along with models for handbags, slippers, and hats for men.

Cotton thread, coil yarn (Scottish thread on spools), linen, or hemp thread is preferred fabrics for white crochet (insertions, edgings, pads, underwear trimming). Silk, wool as well as chenille yarns were recommended for colorwork and also precious metals threads.

Such early designs would make current crocheters nuts, many of which were not correct. For example, an eight-pointed star could turn out to have only six points. It transforms out that the reader was required to read the sequence and to use the depiction as the most precise guide.

Crochet Supplies

Crochet Hook: The first device you need is a crochet needle. Crochet designs indicate the scale of the hooks you need to use. Your boss will help you determine which hooks to use for your first job.

Scissors: Hold a convenient pair of scissors or tweezers for thread clipping, pump cutting, etc. In a protection situation, make sure to maintain scissors.

Yarn: Yarns can be found in a multitude of weights (strand diameter) as well as fiber material. Employ the yarn indicated in the guidance for the best outcomes.

Make sure to buy all of the yarn you want for a design at the very same time as loads of dye will differ somewhat in coloring, and this will be shown on the completed project.

When in the same design you mix different kinds of yarn, make absolutely sure they are

Gauge: Gage is the amount of stitches per inch (and spaces), as well as the couple of rows for every inch. Gauge is defined in many designs over four inches. Your scale will be the same as the gauge defined in the template so that your project is the right size. That's particularly important for initiatives that need to match.

Think about making a gauge palette again once you start the design. Utilize the same thread, needle, and template stitch as set out in the directions to test the strength. Create a swatch of around 6 inches long. Work around 6 inches in sequence, then attach. And let all the swatch settle a little, then squish it to fit without no stretching.

Use sticks, map off a 4-inch square segment of stitching in the middle of the swatch. Count the amount of stitches as well as rows in this segment of 4 inches. Ye can start immediately in on your design if they fit the scale.

If you've had very few stitches, you're operating too loose— shifting to a small hook and creating another swatch. If you've got just so many stitches, you're working too closely— shifting to a bigger hook.

Continue to make swatches as well as play with hook measurements until you get the required gauge. Different manner, everyone/crochets should help you create a design that suits. Each yarn skein has the size of the yarn and the label's suggested hook. For your future, you'll want to retain the sticker.

Threads are used to knit as well. Crochet yarn is commonly used as a project edge for dollies, place mats, table tops, or table tops. A thread of 10 dimension is the most widely used.

The greater the amount of loops, the better the thread, so finer than 10 is 20, and finer than 20 is 30. You're going to need to use a thread snare to crochet this sort. With a 10-thread dimensions, a "0" hook tends to work well.

Tapestry Needle: For embroidery seams, a blunt spotted sculpture needle is used. It is safer to have a simple, steel needle. Many needles throughout the tapestry have a ridge around the neck. These aren't perfect for crocheting seams as when the hump traps stitches, which makes it difficult to pull thru the thread.

Measuring Tools: You would need a ruler (6 or 12 inches), a tape, or a metal-measuring gage to measure.

Useful Things To Know About Your Crochet Equipment

Crochet needles come in many shapes and patterns, but how do you select right one?

Sizes

A crochet needle's size is generally determined by a measurement of length, number, or ' mm. ' If they are defined by text, for example, they tend to range between E to J – E becoming the lowest as well as J being the highest.

Yarn

Each crochet needle is designed to operate with a distinct yarn type; the image below shows the weights that work with those of the hooks.

Hook Size	UK Yarn Weight
2.5mm – 3.5mm hook	4 Ply Yarn
3.5mm – 4.5mm hook	Double Knitting (DK) Yarn
5mm – 6mm hook	Aran Yarn
7mm and larger	Chunky Yarn

A standard G or H needle (the mid-range one) with such a DK weight yarn is typically used by beginners.

Crochet Goal

Crochet fans are looking forward to finishing crochet creations, which are usually useful, desirable, or helpful items in certain way. Popular designs involve Afghans, crocheted blankets, baby booties, scarves, caps, and squares of granny, shawls, belts, tote bags, and many others. A range of different items can be crocheted, from hats, shoes, and curtains.

It is also necessary to use different components in other products. Crochet trims as well as edgings, for instance, are common projects; you may attach these to crocheted products, knitted items, including sewn pieces (including ready-made supermarket-bought items), such as purchasing some shoes, towels, and pillow cases, and applying a crocheted finish to the whole.

Techniques for crochet are also common activities.

Not very many crocheters are obsessed about crochet tasks being done. In addition to the tasks, there are many other objectives, objectives, and incentives of crochet.

The Crochet Base Unit: A Crochet Sew Every crochet design comprises of crochet stitches. The following are the fundamental crochet stitches:

- The chain stitch

- The slip stitch

- The single crochet stitch

- The double crochet stitch

- The half-double crochet stitch

- The treble crochet stitch

- The double-treble crochet stitch

- The triple-treble crochet stitch

Crochet Stitch Patterns

To create unique stitch designs, crochet fans may adapt the simple stitches in unique ways. Multiple different looks can be created; lacy or flat, decorative or translucent, patterned, or simple stitch designs can be used. Many common patterns of crochet stitches are about as follows:

- Shell stitch

- V stitch

- Cluster stitch

Crochet Patterns

A crochet trend is a collection of crocheting guidance for an item, or a connected set of materials at times.

Where to Find Crochet Patterns

There are many locations where you can locate crochet designs. There are plenty of trends available on the web for download.

There are also several crochet designs available on the market.

There are crochet publications as this, as well as art magazines and articles of overall interest that crochet designs also are contained.

How to Read a Crochet Pattern

Crochet designs typically use acronyms to write their designs to save paper. You need to comprehend that and reacquaint yourself with that of the acronyms included within the pattern in order to understand a crochet model.

Typically in a sensible place, you will be able to locate the acronyms. We put the acronyms near the top within each pattern before the instructions with the patterns we posted on our website.

If the template was from a publication or journal, you can typically find the acronyms mentioned at the front or rear of the paper elsewhere.

Similarities and Differences between Crochet and Knitting

There is often ambiguity about crochet and knitting. The methods share some common aspects; for example, wool is used by both crocheters as well as knitters to construct each designs.

Different sorts of designs can be made using either method: afghans, shawls, caps, scarves, etc. You could tell at a glance how well an individual is knitting or crocheting from looking at the materials they are using.

When (s)he uses a pin, (s)he crochets; when she uses two pointing needles, or maybe a wounded knitting stitch, (s)he knits.

Who Can Crochet? Could You? Is Crochet the Right Hobby for You?

If you have never crocheted since, you may shudder to think if it's a meaningful leisure activity, or whether it's something you'd want to get engaged with. Will crocheting require particular talent?

The good news: you can crochet, just about anybody's thing is crocheting. There have been young kids crocheting, as well as incredibly old men. Both the crocheting of males and females. Folks from around the globe crochet.

Disabled people are crocheting, and even blinded people are engaged. People who are poor are crocheting, and so are the rich.

To crocheting, there are almost no disincentives, but you may want to be conscious of a few imperatives before you begin.

Basic Crochet Stitches

Holding the yarn and hook

The nicest way of holding the hook as well as yarn, there have been no hard rules. Go for the most pleasant way you like.

Most people would prefer the "grip of the pen." The needle is kept as if gripping a pencil in the hand while holding.

Many individuals would prefer the "grip of the knife." The tool is kept in the hand while holding as if you were holding a knife for supper.

You can find it beneficial to loop the yarn across the fingertips of that same hand, opposing the one keeping the hook to retain the mild tension throughout the yarn required for simple, straight stitches.

Choose one of these methods, or find a different way that will make you feel relaxed.

The left hand keeps the job then manages the thread's stress at the very same time. The left longest finger is being used to treat the yarn, whereas the index finger with thumb keep over to the task.

Many individuals find it much more convenient to use the forefinger to maneuver the yarn then keep the object with the middle fingers and thumb. When one method feels uncomfortable, look at other ways when you're studying before you discover the one which fits you.

Slipknot

Whatever you crochet, you're going, to begin with only a slip-knot. Because that's how the yarn is connected to the hook at first.

- Make a sequence close to the yarn's tail end. Using your snare or fingers to draw thru the loop, the yarn from just the ball.

- Put its hook loop as well as pull all ends of the yarn (the tail end as well as the working end) to render the hook snug. Need not draw it too close; you must be able to crawl the needle thru the loop.

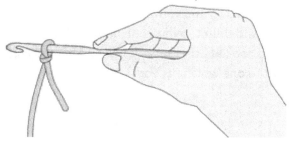

Yarn Over

You will have to tie the yarn across the hook or even draw it over an established weave or slipknot to allow crochet stitches. Which means you are going to create a yarn on every stitch you're making— and maybe some stitches include more than a yarn. Practicing it is a great skill.

- Tie the yarn around then over the hook also carry it towards the front of the hook with both the slipknot on the loop as well as the functioning yarn at the rear of the handle.
- Throughout the curvature of the needle, pick up the operating yarn, and then you will be prepared to pull this through the braid or stitch to make a new stitch. Use the needle to pick up the yarn, instead of using your hands to place the yarn across the hook.

  And allow the hook do that work! This will be easier, and there would be even more pressure into your stitches.

Foundation Chain

You've created a slipknot, so you know what to do about a thread. Okay, with the foundation line, crochet truly begins. A stitch of the chain is a thread shaped to your ring. Chain a number of these grooves or chain stitches, and now you've got what's called foundation chain.

A crochet template can instruct you how often chain stitches your base chain needs to make. It might just be a few — or an only several hundreds! You will then fit into the base chain stitches with other stitches, including individual or dual crochet stitches.

- Form a slipknot on the back end from your yarn to begin your chain then put that on your string.
- Keep the loop in your main hand while holding the thread in your other hand. Using your middle as well as thumb to retain the pleat as well as tail end firmly; have both the yarn's working end all over your lengthened forefinger.

  First, you can loop your pinky finger across the functioning yarn to allow you extra friction onto the thread.

- Yarn during the first link stitch and put the thread thru the hooks slipknot, establishing a new connection line. That's the first thread of your row. (Do not include into your eventual stitch number the beginning slipknot.)

- Iterate the third step to allow the amount of stitches throughout the chain.

Turning Chains

Chains stitches are often used to create a spinning chain at just the end of crochet lines, which is shortened as "tch." Prior to changing the job, the template must instruct you to produce a given amount of chain stitches.

The larger the strokes you make, more and more stitches you are usually urged to make. For starters, you would need one spinning chain stitch for a sole crochet. You're going to have two chain stitches with half-double crochet.

You would need two to three stitching for dual crochet; you will need three to four stitching for treble crochet. Such chain stitches are produced the exact the same with the base chain you've been operating on.

Slip Stitch

For the round crocheting, a slipping stitch is being used to connect the edges of your base chain in a loop or circle. Or you could use a slipping stitch to shift your functioning yarn then hook to another place in your job by breaking the yarn while touching it.

- Embed the hook between the fronts and back in to the first chain from your hook.
- Take the yarn to function from just the top of the loop. Pick up the thread from the hook's curve and move it across the loop of the rope. You now have a hook loop as well as a stitch slipped.

- Iterate steps 1 as well as 2 till the maximum amount of stitches has been slipped as indicated in the template.
- Embed the hook onto the stitch farthest from employed hook as well as operate the slip stitch as outlined above to follow the base chain into a round circle.

Single Crochet

This has been the most common stitch for the design of fabrics. It allows a dense cloth with little or no shifting or sharing, making it ideal for tightly stuffed crocheted animals.

- Perform the amount of chain stitches defined to build a base thread. Switch the job around, so you're primed for the chain that you have already just created to build back.

- You will bypass a chain stitch (a turn chain) for a sole crochet as well as attach the hook back and forth within the coming chain on only the hook. Drag the thread thru the chain stitch and loop over the handle.

- You're going to have 2 hook loops now. Drag the hook into both knots on both the hook then rope over most of the line.

- You're going to have a loop available on the line. Kudos — you only accomplished a single/simple crochet stitch.

Single Crochet on Subsequent Rows

Loop one (turning loop) when you've finished a simple crochet row and transform your job around. What is it? The finished row would not appear really like the chain of the base. Yet look carefully, and then you'll find the sections you've already created of that same stitches.

For performing the following row of sole crochet, you just have to choose to operate out of the front loop, either a line loop or just the rear loop.

Some patterns determine only when to work via the main or rear loop; when nothing is defined, all loops operate.

Double Crochet

Dual crochet is bigger than solo crochet, allowing a yarn that is smoother and more durable.

- Work double crochet in a base line, thread over loop, bypass 2 or 3 chain stitches (based about whether the design needs two or three rotating chains) and move the hook between the front and rear into the next row.

- Fasten the loop throughout the ring and bring thru the thread of the link. You're going to have 3 hook links. Then rope as well as draw the thread through 2 of the hook's loops. Here you will have 2 loops on only the hook now.

- Fasten over the hook then draw the hook thru those two hook grooves. You've now finished a dual crochet stitch as well as on the needle; you have a loop.

- Fasten the thread over the handle, drop the curve into the following chain stitch as well as perform measures 2 or even 3 to create dual crochet stitches.

Double Crochet on Subsequent Rows

Also, for sole crochet, operate the required amount of spinning chains until you come to the end of that same base chain and then change your job. Yarn over thread, place the hook in to the stitch's assigned portion (front, rear, or both grooves), and function dual crochet stitches just mentioned earlier across the lines.

Half-Double Crochet

This stitch, however, is midway between both the two due to firmness and versatility, wider than sole crochet, but smaller than dual crochet.

- Apply in the base thread, yarn across the loop, then move the hook between the front then back of the line in to the 3rd chain (this turning chain is the very first two chain strokes). Once more thread over loop, draw the hook thru the stitch of the link. You're going to just have 3 hook chains.

- Fasten the line over it and push the chain throughout all three thread loops. You have quite a half-double stitch and a thread on the needle.

Half-Double Crochet on Subsequent Rows

Once you reach the limit of the base chain, operate the required amount of turning strings, also for sole and then dual crochet, and then switch your job around.

Yarn over thread, put the hook in to the stitch's assigned portion (front, rear, or both loops), then operate half-double stitches as stated earlier.

Triple (or Treble) Crochet

Triple (also regarded as treble) crochet, the largest of the simple crochet design stitches, creates a very durable cloth, including stitch gaps.

- Triple, as well as treble crochet in the Americas, are synonymous terms. The expression "treble crochet" seems to be the phrase used in the United States for much of what we call "double crochet" in England, Australia, as well as other European nations. So remain on your feet and take the time to read your chart.

- To work inside a base chain, thread across hook two times, bypass the very first 3 or 4 chain stitches (based on amount of turned stitches needed in your trend), so thread the hook in the following stitch in the base chain from the front to the back.

- Fasten the loop around the ring and draw thru the thread of the chain. You're going to have four line chains. Yarn again and bring two of both the loops thru the thread. You're going to have 3 loops onto the hook.

- Fasten the line over it and put the chain between two of the thread loops. You're going to have two loops left Yarn over hook and drag the line into two loops left.

  You get a triple crochet stitch as well as a thread on your needle.

Crochet Increases

In order to increase its width of a simple crochet cloth, at the point defined throughout the project guidelines, 2 or even more stitches must be woven into 1 thread.

Render, as usual, a dual crochet thread. So create a new dual crochet stitch in the very same spot—that means you've had a stitch from the first section, you've got another now.

Crochet Decreases

Two or maybe more stitches must be operated with each other to reduce the breadth of a simple cloth by placing the last chain of each thread on both the hook and then taking them off with each other. In this manner, dual crochet stitches could be popular.

- Make a thread for all of the following two stitches to reduce in dual crochet.

- Drag the thread on just the hook throughout all 3 lines.

Invisible Decrease Method

This is a way to decrease stitches and not creating into your crochet small openings or lumps. It is termed the "invisible reduction," which allows you to put the hook into only one section of that same stitch rather than the entire stitch.

It indicates it portion of just the stitch whenever this form applies to "loops."

Plug the thread in the main stitch's main loop (two link loops).

Put the hook through the following stitch's front loop. For this, beforehand, swing the needle down so that you can plug the hook underneath the main loop.

Fasten Off

Split the yarn from an 8 "end (longer when you have to stitch bits together) and attach the yarn securely. Bring the finishing of that same yarn thru the hook loop and twist softly.

Rolling Yarn into a Ball That can be pulled From Center

Many yarns range in hanks, and others are fore-wound as well as the middle pulls.

It is a great skill to choose to roll a ball which really draws from the middle.

- When you pull a ball out of a hank of wool, untie that hank gently, hold this in the big loop. Get someone to retain that for you, or fasten the string over a furniture's back or your knees while curved.
- Wrap the yarn through 3 fingers quite roughly 10-12 times, keeping that loose end of that same thread tight from your thumb.

- Slide the yarn from your hands and keep it strongly in the middle with the loose dangling end of that same yarn.

- Then tie the yarn across the section that you twisted around 10-12 cycles to your fingertips. Once you hold the yarn so firmly, when you're about to knit and crochet, it won't be pulling away from just the middle of the thread, and it could take the stretch out of another yarn as well. Do not grab the outer sheath whereas the thread is tied.

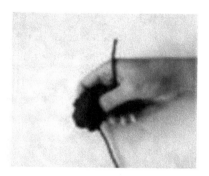

- Keep the thumb onto the position in which the free final part of that same yarn is going to come out to your hands are still on the opposing side now that you've created the foundation to your ball. (We'll label the full side from your thumb as well as the base side from your thumb.) Hold the outer sheath of the yarn with your own finger in the palms.

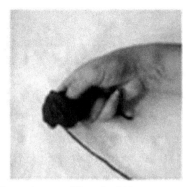

- Then, from the edge, softly wind the yarn towards you, around the ring, holding the thread tight with your thumb. Continue moving the ball against the right to left slowly.

Be really careful about keeping your index finger in the hole that you are forming as you ramp as well as keep the embroidery thread free end. Be certain that you are liberally winding the ball. Just go up and down— not around sides.

Press it more closely around thumb as well as fingers when the ball is becoming too fond of pointing to the bottom.

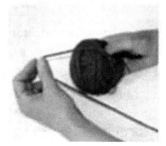

- Dip the end under a few thread loops whenever the thread is all twisted. The spare end that you keep throughout the palm can come out quickly when you're about to crochet as well as the ball won't roll backwards

Crocheting - Attaching In New Yarn

Keep operating yarn unless 2 loops from the ending stitch exist in the operating yarn or colour as you join the new wool or adjust color.

- Pour in the new wool color and draw thru new wool color to conclude the pattern.

- Practice the design directions and continue working the same stitches throughout the fresh yarn colour.

- When you work entire lines in various colors, alter the very last stitch throughout the prior row such that the new color pattern for the following row is prepared to work on the moving chain.

Rather than clipping off the old thread dye, when you are operating a thin stripe template, loosely hold it along the cotton side so that it becomes ready to be picked up the following moment it is required.

It is typically necessary to cut off from the older color or thread for broad stripe designs, allowing a 6 "end to add in. Lengthier carriages are quickly snagged, often known as "floats."

TEACHING A KID

Teaching a toddler to crochet is a rewarding revel in that could have lifelong blessings for the budding crafter.

A lot of us discovered to crochet at a completely younger age, and despite the fact that we would have dropped it for years at a time, the craft caught round in our reminiscences as something useful.

With advantages in each the fast-term and lengthy-time period, it is a talent worth taking the time to train children of almost any age. However, just how do you move approximately coaching an infant to crochet?

Why Educate an Infant To Crochet: The Advantages

There are a few immediate benefits to teaching an infant to crochet, now not the least of which is that it gives them something thrilling to occupy their hours. Only some short-time period blessings of crocheting include:

Children are capable of specific their creativity in a new way. Even though crochet is a based craft, it's also widely open to interpretation and desire, giving kids ample possibility for self-expression through colour choice and other venture-making selections.

Getting to know to crochet can boost.

First, there is the pleasure of gaining knowledge of the way to do something new. Then there's the opportunity of creating purposeful gadgets for self and others, which brings about a lot of delight.

Crocheting hones motor abilities. Children can also find a hook and yarn craft a touch bit unwieldy at the beginning, but as they exercise it, their motor skills will enhance, and the craft will become simpler.

Crochet also can mean working towards other abilities. Older kids can practice getting to know to examine, following commands, and even simple math via running on crochet styles.

Crochet is an excellent analogue opportunity to spending time on phones, iPads, and other gadgets.

Research is beginning to expose that children's developing brains are significantly impacted by way of too many hours spent on displays.

Reminiscence and interest wane while there may be continually the instant gratification of the internet.

Taking time to crochet facilitates a gradual child down and develop the one's areas of the mind that require offline stimulation.

At what age can a toddler learn how to crochet?

One of the first questions that dad and mom ask earlier than trying to educate an infant to crochet is whether or not or not their child is antique sufficient.

There's no specific age at which a child can learn to crochet, due to path all kids study at specific paces.

That stated, maximum children can learn the fundamentals of crochet around the age of 5, and they can increase to surely working on crochet styles around the age of nine.

The Waldorf curriculum emphasizes handwork and gives a variety of terrific facts about what yarn abilities youngsters are likely to learn excellent at any given age.

That curriculum really begins with knitting, around the age of 6, after which progresses to include numerous years of centred crochet lessons beginning the following year.

STEPS TO TEACHING YOUNGSTERS TO CROCHET

All people crochet of their personal fashion, so the most vital aspect in which you check your personal approach of crochet, and try to break down every step right into a chew-sized chew for a kid to learn.

Experience unfastened to evolve the following steps as a result of your personal fashion and the needs of the child you're coaching:

STEP 1: Allow the child to show it as a hobby first

It's not normally an excellent concept to "force" a craft on a baby. What's going to stay with a toddler so much more than the instructional steps is the actual pleasure discovered in crafting?

Crochet often round your child and be geared up to train him while he first suggests a few interests on his personal. If that interest isn't approaching, you may make materials available or advocate it as an interest amongst different options.

STEP 2: dealing with the materials

Provide children time to get used to the feel of the materials. Kids paintings high-quality with a medium-to-large sized crochet hook (size H or above).

The paintings are great with worsted weight or bulky yarn. You can need to make several crochet hooks and yarn options to be had for the child to choose from.

In case you do, make certain to consist of only the ones so one can facilitate a toddler's easy getting to know (easy yarn in a solid, mild colour, hooks with a comfy grip).

Err on the facet of larger is better - huge hooks and fats yarn. For terribly younger kids - or any baby having difficulty the use of a crochet hook - you can need to attempt finger crochet first.

STEP 3: Mastering to chain

The first step for kids mastering a way to crochet is studying to the chain. You can make the slip knot for them and get the hook installation, and you may even make the first few chains to get them going.

From there, it's simply yarned over and pull-through, a repetitive motion that they must practise until they get the grasp of it.

When coaching crochet, you'll need to break everything down into the smallest steps feasible, displaying the child how steps build on every different to result in a completed assignment. For chaining, the steps are

- Yarn over
- seize the yarn with the hook
- Pull through

To teach this, you'll want to sit facet-via-facet with the kid and display the motions, actually displaying every specific part of this step.

Then watch as they practice.do not leap in too speedy to "restore" things as they get the grasp of it but be there to aid them in the event that they ask for help.

Very younger children may benefit from having you place your palms on top of theirs to manual the movement. Older youngsters may additionally find that looking video tutorials enable those to get a better hold close of what to do.

STEP 4: First primary stitch

As soon as an infant has mastered the crochet chain, it is time to learn how to make crochet sew.

Some humans advocate beginning with single crochet sew, at the identical time as others propose beginning with double crochet.

Double crochet is easier in the experience that it is less tough to locate the right location to make your subsequent sew. However, single crochet requires fewer steps to finish the sewing.

Use whichever feels high-quality and strive the opposite if it's now not operating out.

You could need to make the first row of stitches on your child. That is a way of demonstrating the task.

It is also usually less complex to artwork right into a sew (which include the pinnacle of double crochet) than its miles to artwork into a sequence.

Even though you should show an infant the way to artwork thru each loop, it's far extra essential before the entirety that the kid learn how to make the sew than look at the proper placement of the hook.

This is, in particular, authentic for more youthful youngsters.

STEP 5: The Primary Undertaking

Finishing a primary crochet task can simply lend enthusiasm to the craft. A child can complete a task as soon as she has discovered a way to crochet a chain.

Crochet shoelaces or an easy crochet necklace can be made with the simplest a series.

A toddler who has determined out unmarried crochet or double crochet ought to make a square / square tasks that don't require growing or decreasing -potholders and skinny scarves are right alternatives.

FILLING WITHIN THE BLANKS AND SUBSEQUENT STEPS

A toddler can exercise the crochet chain stitch, and they are the first fundamental sew for the long term.

If he stays interested in crochet and wants to hold growing the one's abilities, then it's time to fill in some blanks. This is at the same time as you can pass decrease back and teach the child a few fundamentals that you could have overlooked, which includes:

- persevering
- FILLING within the BLANKS

Next STEPS

A little one can practice the crochet chain sew and their first easy sew for a long time.

If he remains interested in crochet and desires to preserve growing those abilities, then it is time to fill in some blanks.

This is even as you can move once more and educate the kid some basics that you would possibly have not noted, such as:

- A way to make a slip knot on your crochet hook.
- The way to paintings stitches into the chain.
- What a turning chain is and a way to use it.
- The anatomy of the main stitch which is (front and back loop)

After studying those gadgets, the kid can move immediately to observe different primary crochet stitches (unmarried crochet, half of the double crochet, double crochet and treble crochet).

Whilst prepared, a toddler also can want to learn how to crochet inside the spherical or a way to boom/decrease to collect shaping.

Alternatively, a toddler may additionally want to discover ways to change hues. Make sure to show the kid how every new skill builds at the skills she's already advanced as a way to make getting to know more seamless.

EXTRA GUIDE ONLINE FOR COACHING CHILDREN AND BEGINNERS TO CROCHET

Right here are some different matters to preserve in thoughts as you teach a little one to crochet:

Adapt! You may always use an on-line crochet hook. However, your infant may match better with one; this is tapered.

You could keep the hook like a knife on the same time as your infant works fine, keeping it like a pencil.

Attempt out precise yarn options and hook sizes. Show your toddler that there are extraordinary strategies to crochet, and they're all adequate!

Use the dominant hand that your infant might be using. In case you're right-passed and so is your child, then coaching them manner displaying them what you already do.

However, in case you're right-exceeded and your little one is left-surpassed, then you definitely want to alter. Your infant will need to observe left-exceeded crochet.

You could studies it yourself or get help from a friend or aid to illustrate what crochet will appear like the usage of this "different hand."

Use age-appropriate words that the kid already knows. Do you hold in mind the primary time which you checked out a crochet sample, and it seemed like you had been studying an entirely new language?

Keep in mind that befuddlement while talking approximately crochet with children.

Whilst coaching children to tie shoelaces, we often use the "over, beneath and via - Bunny Ears technique," and you may use comparable language even as teaching more youthful children how to crochet.

The Craft Yarn Council suggests talking approximately "fat worms" and "hungry worms" when relating to how tight a crochet chain is; this could make more feeling to kids than speak to me approximately yarn anxiety!

Maintain the yarn in your toddler. Coronary heart Hook Homemakers the extraordinary notion that you can keep the running yarn to your child as he first learns and deeply understands how to work the crochet stitches.

This relieves the difficult step of gaining knowledge of a way to hold the yarn and create the proper anxiety until he is gotten a hold close on the number one part of the lesson.

Be patient.
The point of the workout is for both of you to have amusing crocheting. If you are becoming beaten or confused out via the coaching procedure, take a 2d to compose yourself and locate that joy.

Praise, reward.
The advantages of crochet regularly come from feeling revolutionary and effective, so make sure to reward all efforts via the manner of the kid.

THE Teacher Is Growing Education Competencies.

Maximum of us have favoured teachers and may recollect private tendencies, which made them top-notch instructors.

Actually, the right teacher is familiar with how humans research, remains in rate, is properly organized, and makes it fun through the session at the same time.

How will you put together yourself to be a fantastic instructor? Of direction, some humans have herbal know-how for teaching, but studying, organizing, and taking element in working with others are some tendencies of an awesome instructor, which can be emulated.

This guide became designed to help you in growing those critical trends, and it's going to offer some useful online tips additionally, and on lines that will help you grow to be the quality teacher, you'll be!

Stay Targeted

The focal point of your beauty wants to be to educate crochet on a given ability level.

If university students are beginners, maintain the point of interest in starting abilities chosen for that lesson. They will be struggling to preserve the crochet hook and looking for to bear in mind the manner to maintain the yarn.

While giving instruction, pause frequently to permit the child to remember what you've got just stated. Communicate clearly and slowly.

Talking slowly will permit your thoughts to artwork in advance of what you are announcing, and you may be a lot less likely to overlook something.

It's far continuously an extraordinary concept to make a brief define of factors you want to cover in magnificence every day. There is no alternative for a graphite memory.

WRITE IT DOWN!
Be prepared and organized

Appropriate enterprise is essential to appropriate education and could make you extra green and powerful.

Whether or not or not throughout planning or in the have a look at the room, commercial enterprise corporation is an important issue in a fulfilment teaching.

Assessment and observe for each lesson; collect examples and factors to ensure that each magnificence begins on time and is going without problems.

Being geared up avoids useless confusion, places university college students relaxed, and prepares them for learning.

Be very well familiar with the trouble. Earlier than every elegance assessment, every ability and idea to examine.

Visible aids will help you to your training and simplify your challenge as a trainer. We have all heard, "A photograph is actually well worth a thousand phrases," and that is mainly real teaching kids in a classroom putting.

University college students opt to see what you are talking approximately in the region of clearly taking note of about it.

Lesson Plans

A lesson plan is genuinely an outline of what you intend to train in a category. Developing a lesson plan makes you popularity on how to accomplish your teaching targets for each class and allows you to stay on time table.

If you are jotting down lesson plans for the primary time, beneath are three useful hints:

Outline your purpose for the complete collection of schooling. This may be completing an easy challenge or coaching particular techniques.

Listing all the steps to be included together with your university college students as a way to acquire this aim.

Divide all the steps some of the variety of classes you will be coaching. Even when they use unique lesson plans, you can't usually live on schedule.

You would likely have an entire elegance of gradual beginners, or conversely, a class of fast college students, who complete lesson plans within the time your idea it might take to complete one.

There may be times at the same time as you can simply have to go with the flow, but maximum times you need so that you can persist with your plans.

Maintain Continuity

Crochet is a talent taught in a step-via-step, prepared way. The student has to understand and be capable of making "step" development.

The trainer has to be alert to a pupil's response and be as certain as feasible every step is discovered and used earlier than progressing to the following step.

One education method that can be applied is to offer a hook with rows of crochet already laboured to train novices, skipping the manner to chain till they may be extra adept at handling yarn, hook, or needles. That is an exception to the "Step Rule," however, works for some instructions.

Continuously anticipate college students in a beginning class recognise not anything about the potential; take not anything as a right. Individuals who are self-taught need to comprehend what they are doing right and incorrect.

Regardless of the truth that scholars may have crocheted or knitted for decades, they will nonetheless no longer understand why gauge is vital or how to use gauge information.

Examine moreover offers continuity from elegance to elegance. With the aid of the usage of reviewing at the beginning of each elegance duration and re-capping at the give up of each magnificence, the instructor reinforces the techniques already found out and connects them to new ones.

THE FUNDAMENTALS OF TEACHING CHILDREN NEEDLEWORK

Reflect on consideration on coaching as presenting directed sports activities from which the child will examine.

Learning sports need to attraction to a toddler. Comprehend their modern-day interests and use them to comprise the child in mastering sports.

The kid ought to remember that each mastering pastime leads directly to undertaking the finished challenge. Instance: The chain has to be laboured to begin a mission.

Showing is better than telling.

Demonstrations need to be brief, properly paced and repeated, both by using a teacher or college students.

Demonstrations need to be breached into steps:

Positioned something in their fingers as quickly as possible. The demonstration has to be observed by the learner's doing what they have got found. Kids should have their hook and yarn to try while you're demonstrating.

A completed instance of the undertaking created for kids to examine must be to be had for his or her examination.

The conversation is superior whilst you operate concrete photographs, phrase "pics," and a vocabulary children recognize.

Kids are seldom interested in learning a modern vocabulary simplest for the talent they may be learning.

Children like jokes and games, but those need to be at once associated with gaining knowledge of the capacity being taught. In any other case, they come to be distractions.

Positive grievance and Correction is a critical instructor hobby. Apprehend and inspire any hobby that leads toward carrying out the studying motive.

Display them how the current-day sports activities are related to the completed project.

Children must have an experience of achievement. Offer them with common progress opinions. They may surrender or enjoy.

They cannot do it when they may be not able to recognize development.

While an infant is having troubles doing the demonstrated assignment, display them a possibility, if viable. Repeat demonstration individually the usage of top-notch and new phrases. Study the kid even as he/she tries.

Every child may have a one-of-a-kind "pace," and it may be critical to allow a few youngsters to look at each other step while others are schooling on the preceding one.

Physical putting and sophistication period.

Choose a pleasant area with minimal distractions and a relaxing environment.

The ideal range for a crochet trainer could be 5 or 6 youngsters all jogging on the same challenge.

The extra kids concerned, the greater organization and form is needed.

Example: Small agencies may additionally sit down on the floor and be greater informal, getting up to go back to the teacher.

Larger groups may additionally have assigned regions to artwork and be advised they should stay in these assigned areas, and the teacher goes to them.

Massive groups can be subdivided. Extra adept youngsters might also assist others. However, adult aides are most beneficial.

Teaching Teenagers.

Teach them as adults are taught; however, understand their pursuits are amazing. They want to be handled as adults and now not like "big kids."

Keep away from "dumbing down" the class.

Comprise them in measuring and making plans tasks meeting THE venture of training CHILDREN Keeping.

It amusing youngsters are our destiny crocheters and really worth of our time. Kids need to have amusing and could not tolerate too much seriousness.

They may or might not be inquisitive about "doing it right." Be grateful they're attempting. Do no longer anticipate or call for perfection from kids.

Let them love the learning experience to the extent they may be involved and do not make them experience like failures if they don't accomplish a whole lot.

Often, simply being exposed to the techniques and know-how the concepts is sufficient. If it's been a laugh enjoy for them, they may come back to it later in life; if it hasn't, they may not!

Boys can be more interested in those capabilities than some women, so do now not leave them out.

Ability to associate knit and crochet with their interests: caps and leg heaters for outdoors sports, writing a pattern for themselves with the calculator and tape degree.

As you probable nicely recognize, most kids do now not have a completely long interest span, particularly with regards to doing something that is not very lively like knitting or crocheting.

The task may be simply getting them to take a seat; however, prolonged enough to teach them, so the secret is to keep IT amusing. Go together with the float and do not live too prolonged on a manner to maintain the yarn and hook.

Once they experience at ease, the form will come. Clearly keep them going. Earlier than the entirety, artwork spherical errors and do not rip them out.

Preserve the lessons brief sufficient in order not to lose the child's interest, and before the lesson ends, get them enthusiastic about what they'll research on the subsequent lesson.

If the lesson is simply too long and will become too tough or boring for the child, they may become bored altogether.

Children frequently want to compete. Provide a cause of to them that that is a man or woman learning event and the way rapid or sluggish one does not rely on.

What is crucial is how an awful lot they will be playing it. (This could moreover practice to adults.)

Be affected man or woman, endurance is probably the primary ingredient for success in training, and that is especially real while coaching kids.

So while scheduling your commands, set apart enough time that may be committed completely to the kid/children. Children love interest, and the high-quality one-on-one time you spend with them may be very critical.

As an instance, one instructor who enjoys education, children shows that when coaching young humans, constantly dress quite truly.

Why? One an achievement technique she uses is she sits on the ground with the scholar's popularity in the returned of her. This permits the scholars to look the appropriate way to maintain the needles or hook.

A few college students may still want additional assist. If so, try putting the kid to your lap and, at the same time, as you keep the crochet hook, have the scholar positioned their hands over yours.

It can be time-ingesting, but children appear to in truth like this approach.

Additionally, supply them loads of praise!! (Additionally applicable to adults.) If you lead them to experience fantastic about their artwork, they'll work out greater and development extra rapid.

If you are an education in a class putting, a few youngsters may additionally interrupt others or call for a consistent hobby. Assist them, however, no more than others inside the class.

Be polite, but the company, now not allowing them to "take over" all of your time.

The bodily challenged will provoke you. Most are able to take a look at from you with few modifications on your conventional coaching fashion.

Within the occasion that they have problems hearing or seeing, they will request a seat toward you. With persistence, you'll examine more approximately coaching from those students.

The physical challenged or disabled are eager to research a modern potential and are frequently disregarded from those we'd essentially are in search of as university students.

Do not depart them off of your listing of those who deserve to discover ways to crochet.

There are numerous blind and hearing impaired who educate others. People with analysing handicaps can be remarkably gifted in strategies no longer without issues obvious.

Use these hidden competencies to expand effective needle personnel. Many choose repetition and do very well, analysing needle art.

It may be greater tough to educate your own family or close to friends. They'll no longer take you as severely as different college students and can nice want to apprehend unique strategies.

Preserve your sense of humour and do not feel obligated to offer them the complete direction.

If they need greater information, they will propose that. They will want no shape in any respect. So long as they take a look at, the coaching approach isn't vital.

The maximum crucial component in teaching anybody at any age is that it's a laugh for each you and the pupil, so be innovative.

Time to begin . . .

One professional suggests to REVIEW before starting a brand new capacity or technique constantly. Its miles vital which you be organized and characteristically available all of the coaching aids you need for that training session.

Pre-elegance education may additionally even help refresh your memory on strategies you could not use very frequently.

Pre-class schooling is important whether or no longer you're teaching a large elegance or one-on-one. Ensure you're prepared earlier than you begin a class!!

Many have determined it easier to start through the way of giving beginning college students a crochet hand hook with a few rows of crochet already finished and ready.

Through using this method, university students study the fundamentals of single crochet more effortlessly. Developing a foundation chain in crochet may be tricky for beginners due to their tension.

Once they experience secure with the primary stitches, you may pass once more and educate them the way to start a basis chain.

Its miles extremely vital to include as a lot "one-on-one" teaching within a collection consultation as possible.

A few children won't need to ask questions in front of others due to the fact they do not want others to recognise they do not understand you.

By using on foot across the room at the same time as students are working on a challenge, you may pinpoint individuals who need character help.

But, in no way embarrass all of us with the aid of announcing, "Why didn't you tell me you did not understand.

Patience and tact are vital!

According to another expert, one very critical issue of teaching is giving lots of affirmation.

Continually find something positive to mention to your pupil or students. Word of encouraging like it's "I like the colour of your yarn" or "You hold your crochet hook properly," you will find that announcing something tremendous will help them to acquire correction better.

Hold telling them they're doing first-rate. This will build self-belief inside the infant. They will be happy and feel that they "can learn to try this," if you give them encouragement and fantastic reinforcement.

We have all heard, "An image is really worth 1000 words." it's less difficult in your students to peer what you are talking about in preference to just listening to approximately it.

That is why it's appropriate always to deliver plenty of samples or finished tasks to reveal your college students. Those visible aids can also be used to help youngsters see what different strategies they may be learning.

Pay attention to your students

Concentrate with more than your ears to what your students are telling you.

If their actions are bloodless, bored, or detached, the cause can be they may be simply now not getting your message. They'll be having issues about knowing how pattern or terminology this is new to them. A little extra assist may want to get them to a degree where they experience comfy.

Get students running with their arms as soon as feasible? Discussion can take region even as they paintings. All hand-outs need to be as informative as feasible.

While college students have to forestall to take notes constantly, they lose music of what's taking place in elegance and fall behind with their hand-paintings.

After each class, summarize what become taught in class that day, i.e., casting on, knitting, single crochet, etc. you may then need to "whet their appetite" through telling them what's going to gain knowledge of inside the next class.

always emphasize that exercise will cause them to more relaxed with the yarn and hook in order to in the long run assist them to progress faster

Project tips.

It is very critical that projects be appropriate for the ability stage of the students you're teaching.

The projects that are offered need to capture and preserve the hobby of your younger students. Observe their lead as to what they would really like to create a gift, toy, or garment.

Beginners will want assistance in choosing a sample that is easy and appropriate for his or her talent degree. Bear in mind it is better to grow to be with a completed simple mission than an unfinished tough one. Easy is first-class.

Make the initiatives colourful and attractive to the

Age institution you are running with. Recognize their hobbies and provide projects to be able to encourage a choice to create the challenge.

There are two one-of-a-kind processes you can take in guiding your pupil towards a project.

You can need to select one specific mission for all of your students to paintings on.

Another method is to allow your scholar to pick their personal project. In case you choose this method, have projects that healthy their ability stage and the form of yarn that you will be operating with (worsted or bulky weight for novices).

As soon as you have determined what approach and what initiatives you may use to educate an ability, you're equipped to start your teaching sessions. The subsequent sample magnificence can serve as a model for you.

Recall, modify your coaching periods to the age degree of the kids that you may be teaching. Use the methods that proved to be maximum successful. And a maximum of all...enjoy sharing your talents and talents with a brand new technology!

The teaching of children is the most critical mission. We do it each day in such a lot of methods, without even contemplating the truth that we're coaching.

After they see us doing something, they want to mimic what they see. Allow them to see how a whole lot you experience crocheting and what "fun" matters you could create. Allow them to apply their creativity.

One crucial truth to bear in mind; they're getting to know an ability that may come to be a life-long precious artwork.

You have got the possibility to proportion the present of knowledge with coming generations. Because when patiently spent the time to teach a child now, they, in turn, can be capable of educating some other generation.

Goals for newbie Crochet Classes

BASIC CROCHET METHODS
inclusive of the slip knot and chain sew, single crochet, double crochet, 1/2-double crochet, and triple crochet.

Slip Knot and Chain sew.

Demonstrate clearly and properly the slip knot and chain stitch by way of using a massive hook and bulky yarn or rope.

Also, the usage of posters and corresponding illustrations is helpful when running with a set. Use the sort of methods at some stage in your demonstrations.

Display the two ways to maintain a crochet hook. College students should select the comfiest technique for themselves. Demonstrate the slip knot and how to keep the yarn inside the hand. Have students practice controlling the anxiety with the index finger.

Show the chain sew. Emphasize chaining loosely. Advocate the use of a crochet hook one or two sizes large while working the chain to prevent a decent chain.

Have college students practice making a chain. Provide an explanation for that the chain sew does not be counted as a row. Communicate approximately makes use of for a sequence and display samples of the makes use of, consisting of hair ties or the usage of a sequence to wrap a special present.

Crochet single.

Show a single crochet stitch sample. You can as well use a large hook and thick yarn to show the single crochet pattern. Show how to work in the chain for a single crochet base line and operate under two chain loops.

 Explain chain 1 for single crochet turning. After turning, the first single crochet space working under the two loops at the top of the stitch is always single crochet.

Show a picture, and the double crochet stitch is shown. Explain chain 3 for double crochet turning.

When turning, double crochet under the two loops at the top of the stitch in the second stitch of the previous side. Explain a comparison of the stitch of the shell and popcorn.

Half-two crochets.

Show a prototype, and the half-double crochet stitch is illustrated. Explain chain 2 for half-double crochet turning and not counting on the next row as a loop.

Half-double crochet is sure to insert the hook under the two loops at the top of the stitch in the first stitch of the previous row.

Crochet Triple.

Display a picture and display the stitch of the triple crochet. Explain chain 4 for three-crochet spinning. When turning, triple crochet under the two loops at the top of the stitch in the second stitch of the previous side.

11 ESSENTIAL TOOLS FOR BEGINNERS IN CROCHET.

If you're a beginner looking to finish your crochet tools collection, your search is over. Here we're going to show you 11 important crochet resources you need to start.

It's so much fun to crochet. I love the idea of using a hook and yarn to create intricate designs. Picture the possibilities.

But you need to look at these 11 important crochet devices before you start stitching, which can greatly enhance your arsenal.

Yarn

Shopping for yarn is undoubtedly an exciting interest which could brighten your temper and get you excited for projects.

Yarns are crafted from special materials, so that you may also need to do some studies on which one works excellent to your unique undertaking.

2. Crochet Hooks

Hooks are available in unique sizes and are crafted from special substances. Studies which hook will be paintings first-rate for you.

3. Scissors

Scissors are an important crochet tool that you should never pass without! Much like yarn and crochet hooks, stitching scissors have different types and functions as properly.

4. Darning Needle

In contrast to the usual sewing needle, a darning needle used for crocheting has a large eye for a thread or yarn insertion.

In comparison to a sewing needle, you can insert your thread lots simpler. It's miles used in crocheting the ends of your work collectively.

5. Tape measure

Crocheting is tremendously flexible! Aren't those tape measure covers lovely? We usually see tape measures used for sewing. However, it's a crucial crochet tool to make your crochet project precise, especially if you're following a pattern.

6. Hook Organizer

Together with your cloth, thread, and a needle, you may make this accessible hook organizer! We endorse that you have a hook organizer similar to this to maintain all your crochet hooks so as.

7. Stitch Markers

Stitch markers are cute clips that can be used to mark in which you start and cease your sample. In particular beneficial, if you are operating on a round sample.

CROCHET HOME DECOR STYLES

Crochet domestic decor suits in with almost any fashion of interior design. If you have a bright, minimalistic domestic, a single crochet item can upload a powerful pop of shade.

In case you love eclectic layout, then you definitely may upload crochet in every room. With so much version to be had, you're certain to locate something that provides that perfect contact in your area.

You may additionally flip to those crochet patterns every time which you want to make a housewarming present for someone.

Whether or not it is a blanket to help them feel at ease on their new couch or a wall putting into helping enhance an empty area, those initiatives absolutely upload a personal touch to any home.

1- Crochet Curtain styles

If you want to make an ambitious handmade declaration in any room of the residence, then crochet curtains are the manner to go. You may crochet complete-duration curtains or simply small valances.

Paintings those in filet crochet for a vintage appearance, in ambitious colourings for something greater eclectic, or in a simple, impartial palette for modern areas.

2- Crochet Rug styles

A rug certainly makes a difference in a space. Make a crochet rag rug to expend fabric scraps and upload colour to your house.

Instead, you could make a t-shirt yarn rug or crochet a rug with cotton yarn. Rugs paintings awesome in living rooms, however, may also be used in bedrooms, kitchens, lavatories, and entryways.

3- Crochet Basket patterns

Marie Kondo your house by using organizing the whole lot that sparks joy into handy proper-length boxes. You could crochet the one's bins yourself, starting with baskets in each length. Crochet baskets are commonly made with thick yarn in order that they maintain their form.

4- Crochet Wall Hangings.

Crochet a wall placing for any room of the residence. A sequence of small ones can work well in a hallway. A massive announcement piece appears great over a hearth. You would possibly even make a blended-media fibre artwork piece combining crochet, knitting, macramé, and weaving.

However, you can additionally add art to the home by crocheting small motifs then framing them. You may frame crochet mandalas, doilies, and different circle tasks inside of embroidery hoop frames for a fashionable design.

DIFFERENT KITCHEN CROCHET STYLES.

You may use crochet curtains, rugs, and baskets in any room in the house, including the kitchen. But, there are also other objects that you would possibly crochet for the kitchen best. Crochet adds a homey contact to the house, and the kitchen might be the distance in which you want that maximum. You might be interested in:

- Unfastened Crochet protect your desk from drink jewellery while also making it prettier.
- Loose Crochet Dishcloth Patterns use to assist in make cleaning up around the kitchen a chunk more fun.

- Loose Crochet hot Pad and Trivet patterns to apply on the table and at the counter.
- Unfastened Crochet Placemat Patterns to pretty up the table.
- Free Crochet Potholder styles that are practical, however, also make a stunning wall show.
- Lose Crochet Scrubby Patterns for doing dishes and cleaning the stovetop.
- Free Crochet Teapot comfortable styles for to warm up your kitchen.

OTHER BEDROOM CROCHET STYLES

Crochet can beautify the cosiness of any bedroom. The first location you will want initially with crochet Afghans.

Make crochet infant blankets to enhance nurseries. Upload a crochet quilt in your own mattress. Then put stacks of crochet blankets in the guest room.

You would possibly also want to crochet pillows and cushions for the bedroom. Those accent decor pieces also work nicely on couches within the living room.

Crochet domestic Decor for the bathroom

You may use small bits of yarn to add a costly touch on your bathroom. Crochet soap savers, face cloths, washcloths, tub mats, and towels are all perfect locations to start.

Those all make incredible presents as well. You may also location a crochet doily underneath a candle show for a spa enjoy.

Extra Crochet home Decor styles.

There are a good number of ways that you could upload crochet to the home, such as:

- Dangle a crochet wreath on a door or wall.
- Beautify with seasonal crochet adorns.
- Make and fly a crochet American flag.
- String motifs into crochet bunting.
- Make a set of some items for a themed show.
- Crochet a vase and/or crochet a bouquet of plant life.
- Make crochet mobile phone cozies and other gadget covers.

FOR BEGINNERS, EASY CROCHET STYLES.

One of the great crochet stuff is that even beginners can make realistic, lovely portions.

You simply want to grasp the basics of crochet (consisting of slip stitch, crochet twine, and single crochet sew) to make a huge range of designs.

Simple rectangular shapes are all crochet scarves, blankets, and some shawls.

They don't need you to discover ways to the growth and decrease superior newbie crochet abilities. It is why we protected a lot of the ones in this roundup, in addition to some different fun and easy crochet projects.

Further to the maximum common stitches, it allows beginners in crochet getting to know half of a crochet within the round.

Also, if you are an advanced crocheter, don't be discouraged from those tasks. Such designs are ideal for crochet meditation, rest, and creating gratification immediately.

Clean lose Patter single Crochet Washcloth.

Begin with the fundamentals— single crochet. Paintings it inside the proper length in rows, and you have were given a washcloth. There is also a video tutorial for this sample to help you along with the manner.

Loose sample collection for simple crochet washcloth.

Right here's another crochet washcloth alternative. This one offers with single crochet stitches as well as double crochet stitches.

Unfastened hand towel pattern for crochet. All by way of yourself, you could without difficulty create a crochet kitchen hand towel without much stress using the equal techniques wanted for washcloths or dishcloths! This guide may even encourage you to examine a new pattern.

Clean loose template coffee crochet.

This warm espresso is supposed for beginners. You should be capable of craft one in approximately 10 mins once you get the dangle of it.

They are a tremendous opportunity to coffee cozies that may be recycled, plus they're a tremendous gift idea.

Easy Scrubbie unfastened sample Face Crochet.

To make a cotton face scrubber, use a fundamental crochet circle.

Those are ideal for scrubbing your face and cast off the make-up. A group of scrubbies, particularly if you upload any special cleaning soap to the package, may also make a high-quality gift.

Single crochet and 1/2 double crochet stitches are used on this easy crochet pattern.

Easy, secure sample Crochet telephone.

Device cosies are essentially all rectangles, like mobile cell phone cosies and laptop cosies like this one.

Work them in simple crochet stitches, seam the edges to hold the machine safe, and you have a completed venture that is useful.

Simple unfastened pattern Crochet heart.

Discover ways to use this educational to crochet a small bow. This is a project of three rounds that works truly fast. Unmarried crochet stitches are rounds one and 3.

The shape of the heart comes from the strategic center spherical combination of half double crochet and double crochet stitches.

You may use crochet hearts to add to different tasks as an alternative. Additionally, they make adorable adorn smooth Crochet purse freestyles, card decorations, and patches.

This crochet bag sample isn't always all that different from a comfy sample of a fundamental machine. Add a strap, and you have the precise accent for crocheting.

Simple unfastened baby Blanket sample from Crochet.

Certain, whilst a newbie, you can make a cute crochet blanket! Simplest unmarried crochet stitches and chain stitches are used to construct this loose pattern.

 It has a first-rate texture and craftsmanship is soothing. Plus, you're completing with an assignment you could be happy with! The quick outsized pattern of Blanket headband free Crochet.

Thick double crochet stitches for a cumbersome scarf also are the ideal desire. To make this extra headscarf special, learn how to upload some fringe.

Simple unfastened pattern Crochet Infinity headband.

The scarves of infinity are so named because they are infinite loops that go around and around. This one can be made without difficulty. It really works with single crochet, half double crochet, and stitches with double crochet.

Chain areas create an openwork design. This is mesh-like. This free sample includes statistics to alter the finished headband's size easily.

Clean unfastened pattern Crochet scarf.

This clean crochet headband works up speedy and makes the remaining present ideal. Draw this up with a half-double crochet variant.

Loose Crochet layout for easy fingerless gloves.

You can make those fingerless crochet gloves if you understand a way to treble crochet.

What you have to do is find this simple sew to crochet a rectangle. Then you definitely sew it right into a glove form, leaving area for a thumb hole the way to make a Double Crochet sew.

This form of the stitch is also not unusual, and it is most of the simple stitches you will research when you first begin crocheting early on.

It is a splendid flexible stitch that may be used with crochet in some of the approaches during your adventure.

This publish first teaches you a way to make a double crochet stitch, then indicates you double crochet editions and what you may do with the dc stitch. You'll be amazed to study all of the matters you may do with this crochet stitch, even in case you're an expert crocheter!

Start with the chain of your base.

You want something to healthy in your double crochet stitches (except you choose a double crochet chainless base, to be able to be discussed later in this article).

You must, therefore, start by way of crocheting a foundation chain.

Begin with a knot of the slip.

Then crochet the thread. In case you're running with a crochet sample, the pattern will inform you of the period of your foundation chain.

If you do not like paintings with a sample, you'll crochet a chain to your challenge so long as you want, plus upload two greater stitches.

And expect you need to crochet a skinny headband with ten double crochet stitches across, for example. Build a 10+ 2 (or 12) base chain.

The cause you are adding the greater chains is because they will serve as the primary double crochet you may see in a second.

Yarn Over and Chain add Pin.

Thread thru the hook and insert the hook into the chain. You may insert the hook from your hook into the 1/3 chain on this first sew.

The chains you are lacking are what acts as your row's first double crochet, but this could now not be seen to you until the following stitch is complete.

This is why you're attaching the ones extra chains as stated above to the muse chain, though, because they assist create the chains that grow to be the primary double crochet.

For now, despite the fact that you may really recollect that this is the way you really want to do it, so yarn over and insert the hook into the 1/3 chain from the hook.

Yarn all over again and Pull through

Yarn all another time and then pull the yarn via that 1/3 chain from the hook in which you inserted your hook. If you have completed this step, you want to look three loops to your crochet hook.

Yarn Over and Pull through 2 Loops on Hook

Yarn yet again. Pull the yarn via the first of the three loops to your hook. This will definitely leave two loops on the hook on the end of this step.

Yarn Over and entire the stitch

Yarn over one very last time. Pull through both of the loops, which are probably still on the hook. You have got completed the double crochet stitch.

So that you can recap, double crochet sew is:

- Yarn over.
- Insert hook into wherein you want to area the dc sew.
- Yarn another time.
- Pull thru.
- Yarn all yet again.

- Pull via the number one of 3 loops on hook.
- Yarn yet again.
- Pull through the remaining loops on hook.

That is all there is to it. As soon as you have got completed the number one double crochet stitch, you have to see that it's miles repute to the right of what now appears to be some other double crochet stitch;

It's the stitch that comes to be created whilst you skipped the first three chains because of the reality they serve as the first double crochet stitch of the first row.

Finishing the Row of Double Crochet Stitches

You best want to bypass those first three chains at the very starting of the foundation row. After completing this, you don't need to skip chains.

 So, you may repeat the equal steps mentioned above to your next double crochet. However, you'll be putting the hook into the subsequent stitch that is instantaneous to the left of the present double crochet hook.

You can hold doing this, inclusive of one double crochet stitch in each chain until the end of the row.

Turning Chain of 3.

As defined in step six, you do not need to bypass any chains besides at the very starting of the muse chain, to make that first double crochet of the challenge.

However, whenever that you switch the paintings and begin a today's row, you do want to create a turning chain.

Its miles similar in which you are making the primary double crochet of the row without sincerely doing the stairs of double crochet sew.

To do that, you'll, in reality, chain three.

This will depend on your first dc of that row. Then you can paintings the following double crochet thru doing all of your yarn over and placing into the subsequent stitch.

Jogging Into Front And Back Loops Handiest.
The steps above define a manner to crochet rows of double crochet stitches. But, there are many topics you may alter to create slightly wonderful designs the usage of the double crochet sew.

The easiest of those is that you may crochet your stitches into the front loops only or the once more loops handiest of every row. This may create awesome textures, anxiety, and ribbing options; however, the usage of the identical simple dc sew.

Growing and Lowering (Non-Compulsory)
If you want to crochet gadgets that are not surely square or rectangular, then you definitely are probably going to want to grow and decrease your stitches.

While your growth double crochet, you actually crochet two double crochet stitches into one sew from the row below it.

Whilst you decrease double crochet, you essentially want to make consecutive stitches into one stitch. That is the manner you do this with double crochet:

- Start the double crochet stitch as ordinary. You will undergo all the steps until there are simplest two loops left at the hook (truly before you do the final yarn over.)
- Go away the artwork on the hook, much like its far. Yarn over, insert the hook into the subsequent stitch.

- Paintings as you generally could thru doing a yarn over, pull through, yarn over, pull via first loops on hook, and you can as well yarn over one more time.

- There want to be three loops at the hook. Yarn over and carefully pull the yarn through all three loops.

- This secures the two aspect-with the resource of-aspect double crochet stitches with a not unusual sew on the top, effectively turning them into one double crochet sew to paintings into within the subsequent row.

Chainless foundation for Double Crochet (non-obligatory).

As explained to you in the first step, there is truly a manner to begin your crochet artwork without truly making a basis chain.

You basically comprise the muse chain into the double crochet stitches in one step. That is a greater superior way of starting crochet duties. Many people like chainless foundation stitches because they're extra uniform than working into a series.

Double Crochet (Elective) Around the Posts.

Crochet stitches are commonly laboured from the row below within the top of the stitches.

They can be laboured around the posts, although. Double crochet stitches are a desire; this is very famous.

They're often used to make cables in addition to the fabric, which can be richly textured.

You can do the front post dual crochet and back put up twin crochet, and you may do advanced strategies like fpdc2tog until you learn how to do the ones.

Right here are the instructions for a double crochet stitch in the front publish yarn over.

Insert your front-to-back hook through your work so that you can crochet the post around a state of affairs in your hook's "front."

Yarn and are available via again. Your hook can have three loops. At this point, you are going to keep with regular double crochet commands.

Yarn over and pull via the hook's first of the three loops.

Yarn over and pull on the hook thru the other loops.

A double crochet lower back submit you could be executed the equal manner except you will position the hook within the front of the work across the point in which you need to make the switch from the back of the paintings.

Twin Lace Sewing Techniques

Use simple double crochet stitches hired in the manner defined above, and you may make numerous one of a kind sorts of gadgets.

When you master double crochet, the sector simply opens as much as you; however, the most important purpose why that, so a few of the fine classic designs is and favourite techniques are made with double crochet stitches.

The following methods are based on the double crochet sew: the traditional crochet granny square: there are three double crochet stitches in every cluster in a granny square.

A way to crochet chains and paintings in the spherical is the handiest other stuff you need to understand for this.

Sure shapes of granny crochet: the double crochet is also used for making granny circles, granny triangles, and granny rectangles.

Filet crochet: This notable crochet niche enables you to produce letters and different extraordinary portraits in styles that range from early vintage designs to the maximum modern styles. Its miles made with stitches of double crochet and chain spaces.

V-sew: The v-stitch is every other crochet pattern that uses double crochet sew and crochet chains aggregate. Putting the stitches and chains produces types of "V." that is a famous option for the fashion of the twenty-first century.

Double crochet crossed: whilst the v-sew is a sample that seems like a v, the double crochet crossed (xdc) seems like x's. It's a fantastic easy way to create a cloth that looks harder than executing.

Cluster sew: Clusters, bobbles, and stitches of popcorn may be carried out with different primary stitches, but the double crochet stitch is very not unusual.

Crochet shell stitch: The sewing of the shell also can be rendered in specific heights; however, the stitch of the double crochet shell is most not unusual.

V-sew crochet cowl: The dc v-sew is paired with the stitch of the dc shell.

Clean mandala: several, numerous exclusive sew styles can be used to make crochet mandalas. Nevertheless, the traditional 12 spherical crochet mandala, an easy favourite, is predicated absolutely on double crochet stitches.

WHAT IS THE SINGLE CROCHET FOUNDATION (FSC)?

Bounce ahead with simple single crochet stitches for your crochet— a chainless way to get your venture commenced.

Many crochet styles begin with stitches of the chain, observed by way of a row of simple stitches. However, what if these two steps can be merged into one? This is what the FSC is doing.

This crochet method can also appear complex, and when you first attempt, it could even feel slower, but whilst you exercise it a bit, it makes your foundation chain a lot less difficult.

And even as this tutorial only is going thru the way to make the single crochet version, you could do it with different easy stitches as properly.

An unmarried crochet base or FSC starts off evolved with a series and then incorporates the unmarried crochet, developing factors in a single thread.

The end result is an unmarried crochet first row that appears even higher than the conventional way of starting.

Here are more than one motives to attempt FSC: the primary row of general unmarried crochet often twists and coils as you spot pictured because it's a good sew. Unmarried crochet base gets rid of this trouble.

You do no longer need to artwork all the one's stitches, only to discover which you miscounted for your beginning chain. With FSC, you could upload or remove or without problems.

In case you need to use the conventional technique, you may nonetheless upload on an additional basis single crochet while wanted.

It feels a hint magical to save a step and assemble your paintings in a modern manner. Who does not like that?

Some styles allow you to realize to apply FSC. However, you could use this even for the ones that don't really make certain to test your gauge and use this approach to your swatch.

Even as this suggests the proper-handed manner of making your stitches, you may flip those directions if you're left-passed.

Is it equipped to give it a pass? Clutch some yarn and a crochet hook in a size that matches your yarn!

Start the Row

This is all you need to begin your basis chain of unmarried crochet stitches. In case you had been making foundation double crochet stitches, or any other version, you may want to make greater chain stitches in the beginning.

Make the Chain a part of the stitch.

Insert the hook inside the first chain you made.

Make certain to insert it simply, so it catches both the left of the first chain and the centre of the stitch, which ends inside the subsequent chain. You need to see strands of yarn at the left and one on the proper. This is how you may insert the hook on every occasion.

Yarn over and draw up a loop. This counts as making the chain part of the single muse crochet sew.

Start the unmarried Crochet a part of the stitch
You should have two loops on your hook.

Yarn over and draw up a loop. This is much like the first step in creating single crochet.

You want to have loops for your hook, however.

End the Single Crochet Part Of the Sew

Yarn over and draw the hook thru each loop on your hook. This completes the unmarried crochet.

Get Prepared For the Following Sew

Take a look at your first foundation single crochet.

The stitch you, in reality, drew the loop (at the right issue if you're proper-exceeded) via is the pinnacle of the number one sew and what you will look at whilst counting stitches.

At the opportunity aspect, in an effort to be the bottom, the longer sew is the chain a part of the stitch. This is in which you may insert the hook for the following sew.

Make the next FSC.

Insert the crochet hook into the chain a part of the previous sew.

Over again, make sure to undergo the chain so that you end up with strands at the left component of the hook. It is a bit much less complicated to look each strand as you upload greater stitches.

Repeat the equal steps from the primary sew. A smooth summary of the stitching machine is going like this:

Insert hook, yarn over, and draw up a loop. Yarn over and draw up a loop. Yarn over and draw via both loops.

Eight paintings vertically for your foundation row.

Despite the fact that most crochet works horizontally from right to left (or left to proper if you crochet left-exceeded), proper here, you can work vertically.

It sincerely is due to the truth the muse single crochet manner is extra like making your beginning chain.

Once you make all the FSC stitches you want to finish the row, you could then turn your artwork and begin as traditional working horizontally.

Keep Crocheting Your Task

Now that you have your first basic row of stitches, you can hold on in your pattern.

What you certainly made counts due to the fact the first row of single crochet, so undergo that in mind in case your sample does not direct you to apply FSC stitches.

As you determine, you can possibly observe that this approach moreover makes it easier to locate in which to work as you move. Its crochet, win-win!

AFGHAN CROTCHET SEW.

Afghan stitch is easy to crochet sew made using the Tunisian crochet technique.

Afghan stitch goes by means of way of a selection of various names; a few humans additionally name it "Easy Tunisian stitch." you would possibly stumble upon exceptional names for it as properly.

Afghan sew is suitable for crocheting many unique forms of projects, which incorporates garb, home decor, puppy gadgets, toys, and additional.

Afghan Hooks

There are several exclusive styles of crochet hooks you could use for running afghan sew. One of the most popular is an extended, clean hook, measuring at least10 inches.

Usually, there may be no thumb grip location on an afghan crochet hook. This kind of hook is much like a straight knitting needle as it has the equal type of a stopper at the end.

You could additionally use a round crochet hook, a double-ended crochet hook, or a hook with a bendy extension on the quit.

Afghan sew mission Examples.

There are various special examples of easy crochet initiatives you could make the usage of the afghan stitch.

Whilst you're finished with this academic, you may be geared up to crochet any of these projects, plus many others.

Top left: Crochet a clean kitchen present set in variegated earth-tone colours. The set consists of potholders and a dishcloth, both of which can be laboured in afghan stitch.

The dishcloth, moreover has an edging of the single crochet stitch.

Top proper: this is a near-up photograph of the crochet stitches.

Decrease left: in case you've in no way worked afghan stitch earlier than, this easy afghan stitch potholder is an outstanding first undertaking to try.

Decrease proper: this is a close-up image of the crochet stitches for the potholder.

Crochet the Tunisian Crochet Base Row.

If you are not already relaxed with retaining your Tunisian crochet hook, you can need to practice.

Start Crocheting the Tunisian Crochet Base Row

If you're already familiar with crocheting, this stitch begins with the same beginning you're used to; you start by making a slip knot, and then you work a chain stitch.

Take a cotton yarn skein and a Tunisian crochet hook size J. Chain 30 stitches, then use your finished swatch to create an Afghan stitch potholder like the one pictured when you're finished.

If you're not comfortable holding your crochet hook in Tunisia, you may want to practice it.

Start crocheting the base row of Tunisian Crochet.

If you're already familiar with crocheting, this stitch begins with the same beginning you're used to; you start by making a slip knot, and then you work a chain stitch.

Take a cotton yarn skein and a Tunisian crochet hook size J. Chain 30 stitches, then use your finished swatch to make an Afghan stitch potholder like the one pictured when you're done.

Work In The Front Or The Start Chain Back.

Working at both sides of the chain, you can see that you have the luxury of operating in the front or in the back. In the beginning, working in the back of the chain can be a bit awkward.

If working in the back of the chain, two loops will be left free so you can finish the project easily; you may want to add an edging, whip stitch through those loops, or use the loops for some other finishing technique.

Begin the Forward Pass crochet.

Use the following sequence to draw a loop into the next chain stitch (the second chain from your thread) and insert your hook into the stitch. Wrap the yarn over the hook and catch it with the hook and pull it through the thread of the chain.

Continue for the Forward Pass to Crochet.

First, in the next chain stitch, you must follow the same exact steps again.

You must repeat this process in your starting chain, pulling up a loop in each stitch of the chain until you reach the end of it.

Number the crochet rows in Tunisian.

You've completed the "forward," also known as the "forward pass" when you've pulled up a loop in each chain stitch. There are some crocheters that say you've completed row 1, while others say you've only completed the first part of row 1. When working, keep in mind that when working on this stitch, it's not a good idea to stop in the middle of a row.

If you want to stop working, both the forward and the return passes are better done before you put down the work. With this method, fixing messed up work is simple, but in some cases, it requires ripping back a little further than you might be used to with non-Tunisian crochet.

Next comes the' return,' better known as the' return pass.' You're going to crochet a chain stitch to continue the return pass.

You're used to crocheting a turning chain between rows if you already know how to crochet. Recall that the thread of this chain is not a turning link. You won't turn over your job; you'll keep crocheting with the same side of the work you're facing.

First, you must start to merge two-stitch groups at a time, as follows: wrap your yarn over your hook and pull it through the next two loops on your thread. Repeat, tie the yarn, and pull it through two more loops around your ring.

The Afghan Stitch's full line.

Continue this process until you've been working all over the row back. You're going to be left with a single loop on your hook at the top.

Now it's time for the next row to continue.

In your next section, you can think of the first stitch as already completed. You wouldn't usually count your active loop as a stitch with non-Tunisian crochet. Here is your next row you have to count it as the first thread.

First, find the vertical bar under your crochet hook. You don't want to work on it. You want to work right next to it in the first vertical slot. If you're right-handed, that would normally be on the left side of it immediately; if you're left-handed, you'd more likely look for it on the right side depending on how you're doing your job.

Wrap Over The Loop The Thread.

You will want to loop your yarn over the crochet hook and pull it through the vertical bar after you put your hook into the vertical bar.

Continue to repeat this series of steps until the end of the row.

Repeat the Stitches.

If you appear carefully at the surrender of the row, you'll see that there may be a vertical bar there too.

When you achieve the forestall, you may repeat the identical cross lower back pass tested earlier. First, you chain 1; then, you consolidate groups of loops till you high-quality have one loop final in your crochet hook.

A few crocheters talk over with this as "working the loops off with the useful resource of twos," or without a doubt "running the loops off."

Whole the Go Back Bypass.

Entire the move returned bypass. You have to have a pleasant even row even as it's finished.

Quit Your Afghan Sew

This curling is flawlessly ordinary with afghan sew; that is virtually one of the characteristics of this form of material.

You can discover smart strategies of counteracting the curl with this sort of stitch.

In a few cases, turning into a member of portions collectively once more-to-decrease lower back will do the trick. In different instances, including a prominent edging is sufficient to counteract the curl.

The edging doesn't want to be fancy; it could also be a substantial band of undeniable unmarried crochet.

TUNISIAN KNIT SEW.

Do not let the call fool you. The Tunisian knit sew is not virtually united; it's far definitely crochet sew. It's now best called a knit sew because it looks as if sew (additionally known as a stocking sew) in knitting.

This instructional will train you the way to paintings the Tunisian knit sew, that could be an on-hand sew to recognize in case you'd like your crochet work to resemble knitting.

If you aren't already skilled with Tunisian crochet, you could additionally prefer to discover ways to preserve a Tunisian crochet hook.

Workout This Crochet Stitch

As soon as you have got found out, this sews, be sure to test out more than one amusing responsibilities you can use for working closer to it.

 Hint: The Tunisian knit stitch is a notable stitch for the use of all of the ones beautiful, variegated yarns, which is probably available.

Begin With the Tunisian Crochet Base Row.

There's the first-rate terminology finished to this starting row. Its miles occasionally called the "base row" as well as the "foundation row."

There can be individual names for it as accurately. Rows like this where you're drawing up loops additionally may be called the "forward" or the "in advance skip."

When you have no longer already found out a comfy manner of protective your hooks while you do Tunisian crochet, you may desire to try this first.

To get started, crochet a beginning chain of any duration more than two stitches.

To begin the Tunisian knit sew, you could see paintings into either the front aspect of the decrease lower backside of your beginning chain. It's exceptional to work into the lower back of the beginning chain.

That manner, there is probably loops unfastened to artwork into across the lower part in case you want to function an edging or elaborations for your paintings later. If you test the lower edge of the work in view H, you may see what is supposed by using "loops lose.

Tunisian Knit stitch pass back, reverse, and pass back skip

The subsequent component has several unique possible names. A few humans name it the "go back" or the "cross lower back pass." some humans call it the "reverse" as nicely.

Even as following different designers' patterns built the usage of this stitch, you could find out that some humans name this "row 2" of the work, even as others envision it as being the second 1/2 of row 1.

To finish the return or different pass for the Tunisian knit sew, artwork a sequence sew with the aid of looping the yarn over your hook and pulling it via the last loop in your catch.

Repeat from all the manner across the row until most straightforward one loop stays on your hook. The closing loop at the hook will rely as the first sew in the subsequent row.

Once more, the terminology for this factor of the technique is not standardized. A few people call this "jogging off the loops," or you can look at instructions telling you to "work off the loops by means of twos."

Others talk over with this as "binding off" or "eliminating," this is possibly how a knitter may particular it; there are precise similarities right here to the manner of binding off in knitting.

Running the Knit Stitches in Tunisian Crochet

If you had been going to work the Tunisian smooth stitch, the following step would be to work stitches into the vertical bars all of the way throughout the subsequent row.

You are now not going to do this here, but the vertical bars create an important frame of reference.

There may be a vertical bar underneath your active loop. However, you can't sincerely do anything with that one, so just neglect approximately it and use the subsequent closest vertical bar as your reference factor.

The usage of your crochet hook, you'll pierce the cloth completely thru from the front to lower back, as established in view R, and the spot to do it is straight away to the proper of the vertical bar.

After you have driven your hook through the fabric, yarn over and pull up a loop. In case your hook went in at the suitable spot, the end result will look something like view S.

Continue pulling up loops on this manner all of the manner for the duration of the row. Running more Rows of Tunisian Knit sew.

Subsequent, you could repeat the steps for finishing the return pass/opposite; it's miles precisely the equal proper right here as it end up the first time you possibly did it.

To feature extra rows of the Tunisian knit stitch, virtually preserve repeating the steps you already found out.

After you parent the reverse, the paintings will look something like view. Then preserve with drawing up every other row of loops and working them off via twos. Now you're geared up to do the Tunisian knit sew like a professional

WHERE TO PLACE THE STITCHES

The other important thing you really need to remember is where to place the stitches from a crochet symbol map.

You're going to work as usual row-by-row or round-by-round, reading photos rather than words. In general, row-based charts are worked from top to bottom, moving in the same direction that you always crochet.

From the inside out, round-based symbol charts are employed from the middle and counter-clockwise (for right-hand crocheters).

Some charts of symbols have row numbers on each row's right side. The symbol chart often has an arrow (usually a solid black arrow) to show you where to start when a circular pattern is being worked.

Unless the picture tells you otherwise, the stitches in a row go side by side (each put into the next stitch).

For instance, the shell stitch symbol may have five vertical lines coming from one stitch; from the row below, you will position all five stitches in the same stitch.

There are usually arrows or other directions attached to the chart to show this when the stitches are to be applied in any direction that is different from the ordinary.

Symbol chart and key included with free crochet pattern over the Rainbow Crochet Snuggle Sack Typically stitches are worked through both loops.

There are exceptions, however, where only in the front loop or back loop stitches are worked. There is a symbol for each of these variations: a half-circle with the open end facing downwards for the back loop or upwards for the front loop (u-shape).

It helps to remember that the stitch for the front loop lies inside u, nearest to you, and further away from you on top of the hump of an inverted u for the back loop.

You will sometimes fit around posts rather than into stitches, of course. As mentioned above, there is a hook at the bottom of the post stitch symbol that indicates this. The hook is wrapping around the post.

Lastly, crochet diagrams typically do not indicate whether you are working in a stitch or between stitches in a chain area.

Although their wide range of example of it but where you'd work in the chain spaces, it's only through additional written instructions or your art experience that you'd know how to work in the chain space rather than in the stitch.

For this purpose, if they are usable, it is important to look at the written instructions.

Tip: "Write" Aloud Charts for Practice When you start working with symbol charts at first, it can help you write each stitch aloud when you work to focus your attention on what you're doing.

Take, for example, Linda Permian's crochet symbol chart for the Small Leaf pattern in the Flowering Necklace free crochet pattern: Looking at this picture of the leaf, you see a series of chain stitches and from your crochet experience, you know this is where you continue.

So, you count the symbols of the chain and find there are nine, and you can say "chain nine" to yourself.

When you reach the end of the nine chains, it's time to start your first row. The first stitch you see is a mark of "x," referring to a single crochet stitch.

There's just one of them. Whenever you look closer at it, you see that this is done away from the hook (where you made the final chain of the nine chain stitches) into the third line.

So, you might say to yourself aloud "single crochet in the hook's third row." First, you see that there are two symbols for half double crochet stitches, so you might say, "The half double crochet in each of the next two links."

Each of the next three chains has a double crochet symbol. Say aloud, "In each of the next three strings, double crochet."

Now take a closer look at what is going on in the chart. In the first chain you made (which is on the left of the work), there are eight double crochet symbols.

All of these are put into that one stitch, and it takes you around to the other side to finish row 1 by working on the opposite side of the foundation chain. For now, tell aloud, "the last series of eight double crochets."

Switch the job so that by working on the opposite side of the foundation chain, you will continue to follow the map. You can see that the work you've already done is a mirror image.

So, you may say aloud, "dual crochet in each of the next three lines, half dual crochet for each of the next two chains, and crochet single in the next section.

Also, this symbol chart should have a slip stitch symbol, though it doesn't. You'd slip stitch to the first single crochet to close the leaf and then fasten off your job.

Extra guidelines for analysing Crochet symbol Charts
Remember to check the pattern key for the image chart before starting the work.

 Although maximum designers use the standard symbols adopted by way of the Craft Yarn Council, a few patterns may use extraordinary stitches, so it's constantly first-rate to double-check.

 Be aware that maximum symbols correspond to US crochet terms, but some patterns, specifically the ones written by way of UK crochet designers, may correspond to UK crochet terms.

Dabbles and Babbles has a clear chart displaying how the symbols correspond to the US vs. united kingdom terms.

Practice operating from charts which have accompanying written instructions.

Folks that already understand how to examine commands can use this as a method of double-checking their paintings as they analyse.

Paintings from the image chart, however, refer back to the written instructions to verify which you're working correctly.

Note the colour of the chart. Commonly, a crochet pattern laboured in rows could have symbols in one shade on right facet rows (frequently black) and in some other colour (blue or crimson, typically) for incorrect facet rows.

WHAT YOU NEED TO KNOW TO BE ABLE TO READ CROCHET SIGNS

As an alternative, you could find that a sample has handiest numbered the right-side rows (the ones which can be worked right to the left in a right-passed sample) or that the proper-facet rows are calibrated very well on the right and the wrong side rows at the left.

• Mark off your rows as you pass. Speaking of keeping the music of where you're in a sample, it could be helpful to mark off the rows as you go so you do not lose song of your vicinity in the paintings.

This could be accomplished with marks at the diagram or by using a row counter.

You could additionally want to apply to sew markers within the physical paintings to track your stitches and rows.

In case you do get lost, appearance carefully at your material and the diagram; they must appear the same as one another, so once in a while, you could locate your area visually.

Notice: although the words are often used interchangeably, there is commonly a difference between crochet charts, crochet graphs, and crochet diagrams.

Charts commonly consult with the image charts mentioned in this text. Graphs commonly check with the block-like visual instructions utilized in niches like filet crochet and tapestry crochet.

Diagrams often seek advice from meeting/layout commands.

Reading crochet patterns can be totally daunting for novices, what with all those letters and numbers looking like hieroglyphics.

But in case you understand how to interrupt your sample down, it is tons simpler to decipher.

Those are the pointers to get you started out — hold them handy, and shortly you will be able to examine any pattern like a seasoned.

Studying a Crochet sample

As soon as you've got selected your sample, sit down, and appearance it over to make sure you absolutely apprehend what the venture needs. Most crochet styles have the subsequent sections:

- An "approximately" section that has sample notes

- Yarn, substances, and notions wished

- Data on gauge, anxiety and/or sizing

- Abbreviations used

- Any special stitches used

These all provide useful (and often important) info you need to know before you start. Allows dig into them a touch extra.

Be aware of which crochet terms are used on this segment, as there are international differences between phrases used in the U.S. and the U.K. You need your pattern to be written within the terminology you're used to.

Yarn, materials, and Notions
Make sure you check vividly to ensure that you have all the yarn and different substances you want.

In case you're the usage of more than one skeins of yarn that have one-of-a-kind dye lot numbers, you have to recognise how to control them to avoid awkward and accidental colour versions.

Gauge

Except you're making a scarf or blanket, usually, always, always make a gauge swatch earlier than you start your venture.

Now you need to test your gauge. First, use a ruler to test how many stitches throughout in shape into 4" (you must have 14).

Then, test what a number of rows healthy into 4" (this has to be 7). In case your numbers are correct, you have got the precise gauge.

In case your gauge is off, there are approaches you could restoration it.

So, you may say aloud, "dual crochet in each of the next three lines, half dual crochet each year for the next two chains, and crochet single in the next section.

Understanding the Crochet

Crochet diagrams are a game-changer. They show you exactly what stitch you're the use of and wherein it goes at a look.

Definitely positioned, a diagram is a chart or schematic of a pattern made of symbols that constitute stitches. As soon as which stitch the symbol represents, there's no stopping you.

Even better: diagrams are created using across the world recognized symbols that corresponded to each sew and guidance. In other phrases, they allow you to crochet in any language.

Commonly, diagrams are used for edging, borders, and for repeating sew patterns. They're also on hand for illustrating what distinct stitch mixtures look like.

For some of the simplest stitches, the graph above displays the symbols. The diagram from which you work should provide a reference, but don't sweat it if it doesn't, the symbols are universal.

What this key tells us is that a stitch is defined by each symbol. And if you really dig deep, it makes sense for the symbols: the dc symbol has one horizontal bar to reveal a yarn over, and the try has two bars for two yarn over.

Often, the symbols are about to scale: single crochet is smaller than a double crochet hook. It means that your diagram is a pretty accurate representation of what it will look like when you're finished.

Working in Rows

First things first: Diagrams are labored from the bottom up and are designed for right-exceeded crocheters unless in any other case, noted.

Allows observe the stitch diagram for Granny stitches Rows above.

• Begin at the lowest left, working your basis chain.

Then, you may paintings row 1, reading the sample from right to left. Then, turn your paintings, and sew across row 2, studying from left to right.

• The stitches stack on top of each different so that you can see what sew to artwork into as you cross up the sample.

• A bracket that has been shown on the right side of the diagram shows the variety of rows within the sample repeat.

How to Read a Crotchet Chart Sign

Crochet instructions can be written in text (with or without abbreviations) and/or graphed or charted in symbols. Reading symbol charts expands your options to work with different crochet pattern types. This guide describes how to interpret the charts of crochet.

What Are The Crochet Symbol Charts?

A Symbol Chart is a visual representation of a crochet pattern. Each row or round is represented using symbols representing the stitches, stitch by stitch. The Council of Craft Yarn has introduced a set of uniform crochet symbols that are widely used across all crochet designs.

The symbols in the chart are designed to look like simple stitch representations; once you've been used to seeing them, they'll be as plain to you as the written crochet abbreviations you see in patterns.

You know "sc" means single crochet, and you'll find out that a symbol ofx or + also means single crochet.

The image above for the five double crochet shell is shown right here within the higher right nook of the stitch.

This image additionally consists of the visible design of the stitches as well as the written commands

Symbol charts, provide a visible opportunity to written commands for crochet symbols. There are numerous motives why this may be useful:

1. Many crafters are visible freshmen. There are numerous one of a kind ways to learn, and a number of human beings find picture-based instructions simpler to recognize than text-based guidelines.

Make the craft easier on yourself if you're a visual learner with the aid of getting to know a way to examine charts.

2. Charts beautify written commands. In many cases, a crochet sample consists of each written and symbol commands.

You could normally discover it smooth to examine text guidelines; however, in some cases, it is able to be helpful to have a look at the visible to make feel of specific portions of the sample.

It's far greater information that may be beneficial.

Three image charts aren't language-based. Once the way to read crochet image charts, you may be capable of observing them on every occasion they're to be had.

This lets in you to get crochet books in different languages (eastern crochet books are popular, for example). You shouldn't know the way to examine the written language in case you share the common language of crochet.

A be-aware for Left-handed Crocheters

As we continue into the info of analysing image charts, it is critical to be aware that maximum charts are written for right-exceeded crocheters.

That the pattern must be reversed for left-surpassed crafters. This can be completed mentally or thru physical reproductions.

HOW TO READ THEM.

When you get acquainted with the symbols that represent every stitch, it is fairly easy to study image charts.

They're designed to read precisely as they look, so the fabric that you are creating on your arms will look similar to the visible diagram on the web page.

There are key things to learn while studying image charts: what the sew is and where it is going.

- There are traces to symbolize "yarn overs." The double crochet sews like the 1/2 double T with a single "hatch" line across the bar.

This line represents that it has one "yarn over" to make the double crochet. The treble crochet seems similar but with two hatch lines representing the 2 "yarn overs" that start this stitch.

- Brackets are used to suggest sew pattern repeats. Many designers additionally encompass the phrase "repeat" to signify the location to repeat and the wide variety of times to achieve this.

- Colours are commonly indicated with the aid of the letter. The Ogee stitch Afghan loose Crochet sample includes a list of materials that indicates which letter corresponds with which shade.

CROCHETING A PICOT STITCH

Typically, the Picot Seam is used as an outline, applied to a completed fabric. Take this guide and start making 3 stitches of picot.

Small Picot Stitch:

1. Operate across a completed item's bottom. (To add a picot side length to something like a ready-to-wear item, start with a sole crochet or dual crochet strip.)

2. Single crochet inside the first stitch.

3. Chain three, single crochet in the subsequent stitch.

4. Single crochet inside the subsequent three stitches. Chain three, unmarried crochet inside the subsequent stitch. (Picot fashioned).

5. Repeat step 4 throughout the row.

Low stitch of Picot:

 1. Follow the tiny picot stitch instructions, but chain five as opposed to chain 3.

3. Do the sequence of unmarried crochet, chain five, single crochet in the same stitch to make a slightly flared picot side as shown in the image to the right one.

3. This could barely pop out and will support the bottoms of tank tops, or skirts, on sleeve edges, or caps.

Crocheting the seeds stich.

This seven-step tutorial shows you how to crochet the stitch of seed. The seed stitch is a single and double crochet stitch that alternates. It offers a closed stitch that looks like a stitch of knitted thread.

- Begin with a chain. Turn, single crochet from the hook in the second stitch.

- Dual crochet in the next stitch.

- Single crochet in the next stitch.

- Iterate steps two as well as three across the row.

- One line of seed stitch accomplished.

- Turn at the end of the line when you ended up in double crochet, the first stitch of single crochet.

Slip stitch in the first line, chain 2, (takes the place of the first double crochet), simple crochet in the next stitch, when you finished in single crochet.

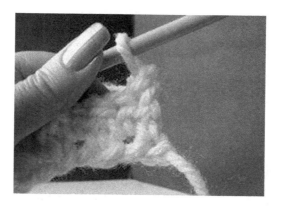

- Go through the row, alternating with a single crochet in the previous row's double crochet, and vice versa. Photo shows 3 rows of completed seed stitch.

A way to crochet inside the spherical shape.

This is a splendid little by little educational that teaches you a way to crochet within the spherical shape.

Steps:

1. Chain a hoop on which to build your crochet inside the round: chain 5, slip stitch to join.

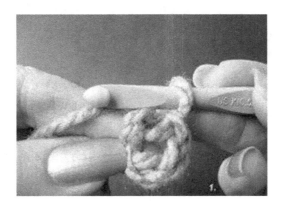

1. Chain 2 to begin to double crochet.

- Consider the number of double crochet stitches needed for the round. 10 Double crochet in this case, plus chain 2...

- Fifth and sixth. Slip to touch the thread. At the beginning of the string, slip stitch into the top of chain 2.

- Chain 2 to begin following round of stitches.

- Switch the job in the opposite way. (You can also spiral crochet in the round, so you don't turn.)

- Finish the crochet stitches needed for that round. (You're going to increase the stitches in each round in about any case.)

- Slip stitch to join the round.

- In attempt to provide an invisible edge, shut that stitch to slip the stitch in.

The arrow points to the right stitch to reach the slip stitch. Slip stitching in the wrong stitch is the most common error in the round's crochet. Image 15's arrow points to the right stitch to reach the slip stitch.

How to Crochet a Checkerboard Stitch

The stitch of the checkerboard is a really good stitch. For a very neat-looking afghan, you can use just one for a dishcloth or knit the squares together. It's a perfect step by step guide to this tutorial.

- Begin with a chain. Dual crochet at the hook's third stitch and at the next stitch

- Chain 3.

- Jump the following three stitches. Make Double crochet in each of the next three seams.

1. Repeat steps 2 and 3 across the row. Always end with a double crochet in the last stitch.

*   Chain 3 and turn.

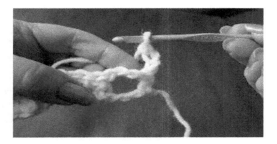

- Create 2 dual crochet in the preceding row's chain 3 room. (Chain 3 is the very first dual crochet instead.)

- Chain three, make three dual crochets in the space of chain 3 of the preceeding row.

2. Repeat step 6 across the row.

3. Photo shows 3 rows of checkerboard stitch completed.

How to crochet a crazy shell stich

Follow this step-by-step guide to learn how to make a mad stitch of mesh. You start with multiples of three in a chain first, but in the tutorial, you can read that. This is a lovely stitch you're going to want to know.

1. Start with a line, plus one extra in multiples of three. 15 + 1, or 18 + 1, or 21 + 1, for instance. Make 3 double crochet from the hook at the 4th stitch.

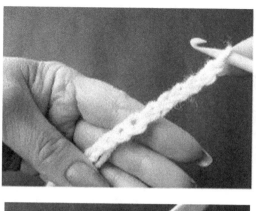

- Leave the three subsequent stitches, sole crochet in the next stitch.

Chain 3

Make 3 double crochet in the same stitch, skip the next 3 stitches, single crochet in the next stitch.

Repeat from * across the row. End with a single crochet.

- Second Line: Chain three and make the turn. Make three dual crochets in the sole crochet of the preceeding row. (The same stitch as the chain three just made.)

Simple crochet in Three place over the next row. (You'll notice it on the opposing side of that same previous row's next dual crochet cluster.)

Chain three, make three dual crochet in the same chain three space. Single crochet in the next chain 3 space.

Repeat from across the row three Repeat the second Row until your achieve the required size of your project.

How to create a pop-corn stitch

It is quite simple when you have the correct instructions on how to do that. All you do is render in the same row a series of dual crochet stitches. This brilliant guide is going to be showing you how.

- Set a set of pillars that can be separated by Three solo crochet from the needle and in every loop of the set in the second thread.

- Chain One then switch, solo crochet over the next Two stitches. Create Five dual crochet stitches over the next row, holding each stitch's last chain on the thread.

- Insert the stitch into all of the six loops on the hook.

- Solo crochet in three subsequent stitches.

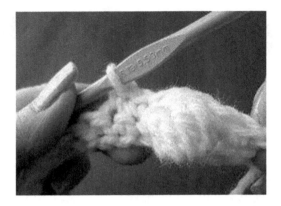

- Iterate steps two, three, then four across the row, beginning the step two.
- Chain 1 and turn, single crochet in each stitch across the row. (In the popcorn stitch, single crochet in the center stitch.)

(Single crochet in the centre stitch of the rear of the popcorn stitch.)

7. Iterate the following steps two, three, four then five for the number of rows required to complete your project

(2 rows of popcorn stitch completed)   (3 rows of popcorn stitch completed.)

How to Crochet a Shell Stitch

To know how to make crochet of a shell stitch, obey this seven-step tutorial. This stitch can then be used in any method you want.

- Begin with a chain.

- Dual crochet it in the third seam taking from hook.

- Make 4 more double crochet stitches in the same stitch.

- Skip the next 3 stitches, make 5 double crochet in the next stitch.

- Repeat step 4 across the row.

- At the end of the row, turn, slip stitch in the first 3 stitches, chain 2, make 4 double crochet in the same stitch. Then repeat step 4 across the row.

- Iterate step six for each following row of the shell stitch.

How to Crochet a Treble Stitch

This guide contains several photos that will support you make a treble stitch. Employ this guide and afterwards teach everyone else to do this pattern.

Steps:

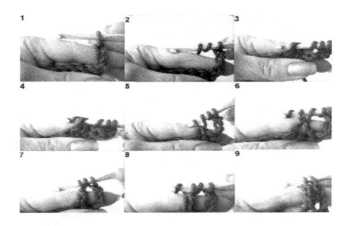

1. To start to make a row of treble crochet, first chain 3.

2. Yarn over the hook 2 times. (3 loops on the hook.)

3. Insert the hook into the next stitch.

4. Hook onto the yarn.

5. Pull through the stitch. (4 loops on the hook.)

6. Hook onto the yarn.

7. Pull through 2 loops. (3 loops remaining on the hook.)

8. Hook onto the yarn.

9. Pull through 2 loops. (2 loops remaining on the hook.

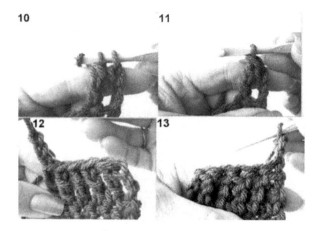

10. Hook onto the yarn.

11. Pull through the last 2 loops on the hook (1 loop remaining on the hook.) Repeat steps from 2 to 11 for each treble crochet.

12. At the end of the row of treble crochet, chain 3.

13. Turn the work to begin working on the next row.

NOTE: Always insert the hook into the second stitch of the row, as the chain 3 is equivalent to the first treble crochet of the row.

How to crochet the magic circle

There are several ways to get around going. The magic circle is one of those ways. You will pull the hole closed by the magic circle. To learn this stitch, follow this tutorial.

There are several ways to get started when crocheting in the round. You can join chain 4, slip stitch, and make a loop.

You can chain three and make double crochet stitches from the hook in the 3rd stitch, or you can continue with the magic circle. In the middle of your work, the first two approaches would leave a hole.

The' Magic Circle' lets you open the closed door.

First, begin in the same way as usual in crochet to make the magic circle.

Create a loop.

Pick up the yarn.

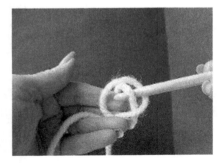

Pull through the first loop.

Pick up the yarn again, to make a chain stitch.

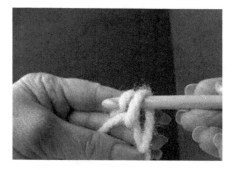

Pull through the loop. (Chain stitch completed.)

Pick up the yarn again to begin a single crochet stitch.

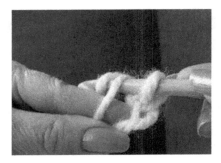

Pull through the loop.

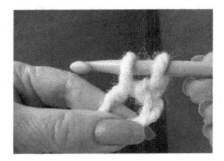

Pick up the yarn again, and finish the single crochet stitch.

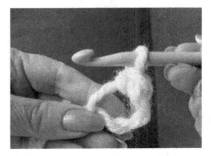

Continue to make single crochet stitches in the main loop.

At the end of the round of single crochet stitches, pull on the yarn end to gather the hole closed, and continue with your pattern.

Photo below shows the magic circle finished, with the hole gathered closed.

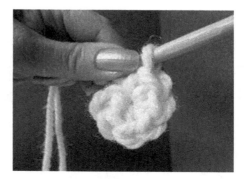

Reverse Single Crochet Stitch-Crab Stitch.

The reverse single crochet stitch for finished projects is a flexible stitch to create a Bouillon bottom.

For the edges of Afghans, place-mats, or other square things that need a more significant edge, you may learn this stitch. This is a tutorial that is easy.

1. After completing a row of single crochet stitches, do not turn.

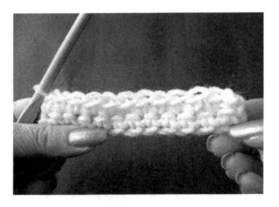

2. Do not turn the work. Insert the hook back into the 2nd last stitch completed.

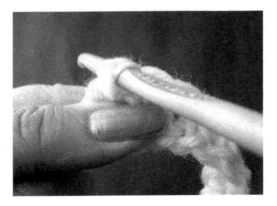

3. Yarn over, and pull through the stitch, just as you would for a single crochet.

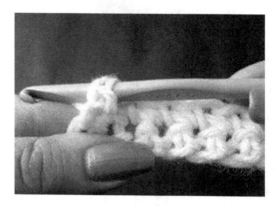

4. Yarn over again, and pull through the two loops on the hook.

5. Insert the hook into the next stitch.

6. Yarn over, and pull through.

1.   Yarn over, and pull through the two loops on the hook.

8. Continue making the reverse single crochet across the row, and the end result is a lovely, coiled style edge to your finished projects.

Tunisian Crochet Stitch.

Many names are known for the Tunisian crochet stitch: Afghan stitch, Railroad knitting, hook, knitting, crochet knitting, shepherd's knitting. To learn the popular Tunisian crochet stitch, follow this step-by-step tutorial.

If you don't have a traditional Tunisian crochet hook, which is a very long-handled crochet hook, then Tunisian crochet is really only practical to make smaller items like wallets, headbands, belts, and other small items that don't require more than a dozen stitches across the line.

That's because all the stitches are staying on the hook, and they're going to fall off the hook's back end!

So, the first chain as many stitches as your project needs to start Tunisian crochet.

Then work back down the chain as if you were making the first half of a single crochet, but keep the loop on the hook as you go down the line. You'll have as many loops on your hook at the end of the line as your chain.

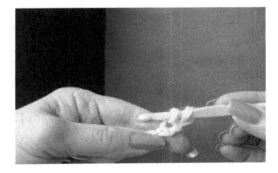

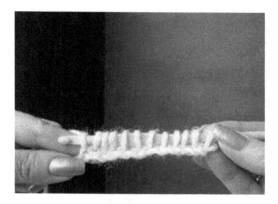

And if you've got a 13-stitch chain, you're going to have 12 line loops.

Now, don't turn the job, yarn over, just pull 2 loops through. Repeat from across the entire row until there is just one loop left on the hook.

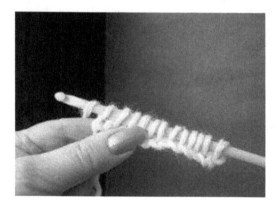

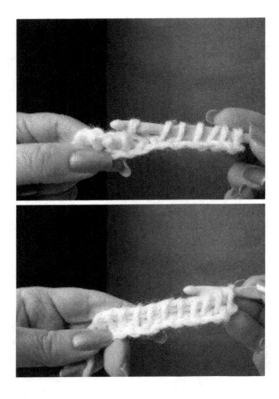

Now, at every point, you're going back down the line, picking up a loop. (Pass the hook through the stitch and go directly to the other side (second picture below).

Count the number of hook loops in each row to establish the proper number of stitches

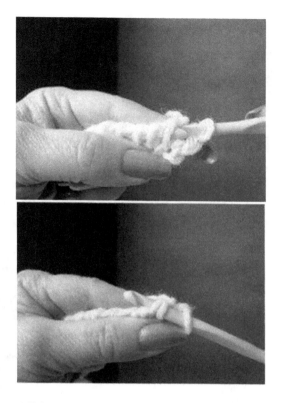

Yarn over, pull forward, keep the loop on the line.

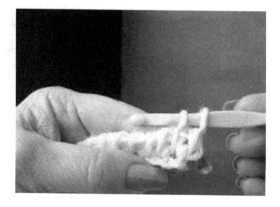

Continue down the row.

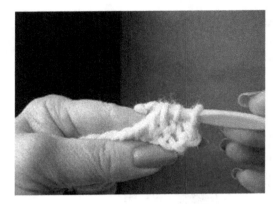

- Four rows of tunisia completed sequentially

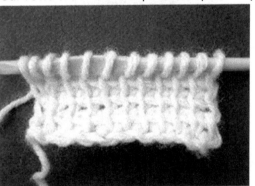

- this is a tunisia snitch been view from the back

Bauble ended picot stitch:

- Follow the commands for the small picot sew, except chain 7 as opposed to chain three.

- Slip stitch from either the hook at the 6th stitch.

- Slip stitch at the chain's last loop. Over the next 3 stitches, solo crochet.

4. Repeat steps one, two and three across the row.

VARIATIONS AMONG KNOTTING AND CROCHETING.

People who are strange with yarn crafting frequently confuse knitting and crochet. It is absolutely understandable that this happens; those crafts share many similarities and not unusual elements. However, they also have big sized differences.

Similarities

Each craft utilizes yarn or fibre, and you could make the equal kinds of projects inclusive of sweaters, shawls, wraps, blankets, Afghans, scarves, hats, mittens, socks, and so on. With either method.

Knitting and crocheting each require similar skill sets: hand-eye coordination, an eye for colour and layout, an affinity for fibre.

The capability to devise an undertaking from start to finish and see it via the mathematical potential is helpful, even though not strictly important, for both craft technique.

Each knitting and crochet offer a number of extremely good health benefits.

Principally, each knitter and crocheters need to have the endurance necessary to maintain running, stitch after stitch after stitch, until a task is finished.

So what is the difference between knitting and crocheting? Why wouldn't it be counted whether or not you do one, or the alternative?

It would not always remember, beyond private choice, of the route, but the ones folks who might just get to know and have a little interested in yarn crafting will want to discover the variations between the two crafts for better information of which one is probably perfect to them.

Right here are some of the each's differences:

Elements
With regards to substances, knitters and crocheters come to be with comparable yet special stashes; you may discover most of the differences inside the equipment department.

Knitting components
A few knitters—hand knitters, this is—use pointy knitting needles. The sharp needles can appear in several unique types of configurations; they often exist in units of, although this is not constantly the case.

From time to time, the two needles are related by using a wire, as in the case of a circular knitting needle.

Now and again they come in units of extra than two. As an instance, double-pointed sock knitting needles regularly come in sets of four or five.

If pointy needles are a part of the manner, then the crafter in query is knitting with the aid of hand.

Hand knitters are simplest a subset of the full quantity of knitters. In addition, handy knitters, there are also looming, knitters and device knitters.

There are numerous unique types of looms and machines that can be used for knitting; they range from the easy to the complex, from the small to the huge.

A few small machines may be used to knit in-wire socks or diverse other small initiatives.

There are larger machines that may be used to knit sweaters, clothes or different similar projects.

Then there are large circular machines, some of which would not even suit in the living room of a median domestic, that mass-produce knitted fabric for the fabric company

Knitting machines promote very well the production of knitted fabrics from very exceptional threads and yarns. As an instance, t-shirt material is normally knitted.

Due to the fact crochet must be achieved by using hand, and it's tedious to apply such first-rate threads for crochet paintings, it is rare to locate crocheted cloth as lightweight and "drapery" as knitted t-blouse cloth.

(That said, there are a few first-rate strategies in crochet that do make it feasible to make crochet t-shirts. It's no longer not possible; it's just something that can be.

Crochet components

Crocheters are not using pointy needles or machines to make their tasks; they use a single crochet hook.

The hook may be small or huge, or any size in among. It'd usually be made from steel, aluminium, and bamboo, plastic, wooden or bone, but it is honestly a nice hook.

Crochet is usually completed with the aid of hand, by no means by means of the gadget. A crocheter's moves are so intricate that, to this point, no one has been able to create a gadget that may reproduction them.

There may be something in the fashion industry. This is referred to as a crochet system, but it does not sincerely make the same stitches like the ones made in crochet.

They devise blanket stitches that mimic crochet; however, upon closer examination, it is simple to peer that it isn't always without doubt crochet.

So, to recap, crochet has executed the usage of an unmarried crochet hook and is usually finished by hand in place of with a gadget.

This, the use of a crochet hook as opposed to needles or a system is what makes the sizeable distinction among the two crafts. But the difference in gear consequences in other variations as nicely.

Yarn

There are numerous distinct styles of yarn, and they can all be used similarly in knitting as in crochet, even though a few fidgety yarns lend themselves better to one craft or the other.

Thread is normally reserved for tiny crochet needles; it is no longer something stated an awful lot in knitting.

There is a long-standing rumour that crochet makes use of up appreciably greater yarn than knitting; however many human beings have tested this, and it remains debatable as to whether or no longer it's far proper.

Structural Differences in Material

There are crucial structural variations between crocheted fabric and knitted material.

Each crochet and knitting has yarn loops that are controlled.

With (weft) knitting (the kind of knitting that's closest to crochet if this kind of part can be said to be), the loops build on each other in a way that requires a few lively loops to stay on the needles.

Every sews rely on the help of the sew beneath it; if a knitter drops a sew, the complete column of stitches underneath it might unravel.

With conventional crochet, there usually are not many lively loops at one time—commonly only one loop, or in all likelihood a few loops.

(There are exceptions to this in a few superior stitches and niches of the crochet along with broomstick lace).

The stitches construct on top of every other, but the energetic loop is the most effective spot from which the fabric is prone to unravelling. So, knitting tends to get to the bottom of extra than crochet; frogging is simpler in crochet than in knitting.

Tasks

Its miles impossible to objectively speak which technique is "higher" for any given form of undertaking.

The fact is, the "pleasant" approach for any given assignment comes right down to private choice. Each of those needlework techniques is well worth mastering, understanding and the usage of.

One motive that this query is so not unusual is that the variations in strategies were lots more mentioned lower back while yarns have been so extraordinary and limited.

The approach of knitting with needles allowed for more drape and a higher match, so humans usually used knitting for clothes and crochet for such things as blankets or desk runners.

That's no longer the case, these days, although, due to the fact the variety of both materials and advanced crochet techniques makes it possible to create all of the identical objects that can be made with knitting.

An awesome example is with socks. Socks was once something best knitters made, but now there are plenty of crochet sock styles.

WHICH IS EASIER?

Ask this question of ten distinct yarn crafters and get ten special responses.

Many humans agree that crochet is an easier craft to examine as it calls for simplest the usage of the dominant hand. But, considering the second one hand is used to help feed the yarn in crochet, it is not this easy.

Many humans do certainly locate that crochet is easier to choose up. But simply as many humans who have tried both crafts discover that it's less difficult to knit.

Humans have a tendency to select one over the opposite after working towards each, but there are also people who revel in each equally. People who strive one and locate it tough may additionally need to attempt the alternative to see if it suits them better.

Knit-Like Crochet

Individuals who aren't acquainted with knitting or crochet typically cannot inform the difference among the two at a look.

Folks that craft in one or both of these forms easily come to understand the stitches which are from knitting and people that may most effective be completed in crochet.

However, the variations among the 2 are more and tougher to discover thanks to a number of strategies that permit crocheters to create knit-like fabric.

Tunisian crochet is the maximum famous of those. Its miles a form of crochet that uses multiple hooks hung on longer hooks (and occasionally even round double-ended hooks!) to create knit-like cloth.

Other approaches to creating knit-like fabric with crochet are via knocking or thru running inside the 0.33 loop in half of the double crochet. After which there are a few crafters who combine knitting and crochet in one item; which includes crocheting an edging on a knit garment.

The opportunities are limitless whether or not you need to include crochet or knitting or each!

A WAY TO CROCHET A HEADSCARF FOR BEGINNERS

Crochet patterns don't get any less complicated than this one! That is pretty much the maximum primary crochet headscarf sample you could ask for, which makes it the proper crochet accent pattern for novices.

Not most effective is that this pattern a smooth way to make a headband; however, it is also written for those who don't have a great experience studying crochet styles.

There are not abbreviations, and there are loads of pointers that will help you alongside the way.

Completed Headband Length

This headscarf measures 84 inches (seven toes) lengthy by way of 4 inches extensive. Scarves can vary in size without changing function, so do not worry if yours isn't quite identical. You may analyze as you pass.

Gauge

Eight crochet stitches = three inches.

While it's tempting to jump proper in and begin making the headscarf, it is desirable to get into the real and genuine habit of checking your gauge.

To try this, crochet a gauge swatch measuring as a minimum four inches square (larger is better).

Make the swatch in single crochet sew the usage of the precise same yarn and crochet hook you'll use to crochet your headscarf.

When you have more than eight stitches in line with three inches, it approaches that your stitches are smaller than deliberate and your headband might be smaller than the example. Try making a brand new swatch with a bigger crochet hook.

Likewise, if you find which you have fewer than eight stitches in step with three inches, it approaches your stitches are large than deliberate.

If so, your scarf is in all likelihood to show out lots longer than intended; you furthermore may chance jogging out of yarn on account that large stitches will burn up extra yarn and create a bigger headband.

Strive to make a new swatch with a smaller crochet hook.

Crochet scarf instructions

Pull out a length of yarn measuring at the least six inches or longer; go away this duration unworked and make a slip knot after that point.

Then, running with the give up attached to the ball of yarn, crochet an extended beginning chain of 224 chain stitches

Row One: paintings a single crochet stitch within the 2d chain from your hook.

After crocheting your chain, you may have a lively loop nevertheless in your hook. Do not count your lively loop. Begin counting with the first chain after the lively loop.

Keep operating single crochet stitches all the way throughout your beginning chain. Work one unmarried crochet sew into each chain stitch till you reach the stop.

Whilst you get to the cease, count the single crochet stitches to make sure you have a total of 223. Again, sew markers are beneficial here.

Next, crochet one chain sew at the top of the row to apply as a turning chain. Then, flip your paintings horizontally so you can see paintings back across the piece.

Row: when you have a look at the top of the row of unmarried crochet stitches you made, you will see that every stitch has loops at the pinnacle. When you paintings your single crochet stitches from this point on, be cautious to paintings through both of those loops collectively.

Working thru each loop, work crochet sew into the remaining unmarried crochet sew you made in row one. Keep running one single crochet sew into every single crochet stitch, all the way across the row.

Make certain to be counted your stitches and make certain you've got 223 stitches in the row.

(Bear in mind to apply to sew markers to help maintain your remember accurate—preserving depend is so important for a hit task!) Paintings one chain stitch on the end of the row and turn the work over so that you can find paintings lower back across once more.

Rows 3 and Up: Repeat Row till your scarf is the desired width. While you crochet the remaining row, do not paintings a turning chain afterwards due to the fact now it is time to complete your paintings rather than turning it over and continuing.

The Way to End Off

Leave duration of yarn at the quit measuring at the least six inches. Reduce the yarn, taking care now not to drop your active loop.

Wrap the cut period of yarn around your hook, grab it with the hook, and pull it all the way via the energetic loop.

Supply it a gentle tug to make sure that it is tight and will not come undone. Thread the reduce give up of this yarn onto a tapestry needle and use it to weave to your ends.

After you weave in each end, you may wear your scarf or deliver it as a gift!

HOW TO CROCHET A DOUBLE TREBLE STITCH (DTR)

Basic crochet stitches include unmarried crochet, double crochet, and treble crochet.

They are among the first stitches novices research, and they're observed in maximum crochet styles.

The use double treble crochet stitch (also known as double triple and abbreviated as DTR) is some other simple sew it really is the subsequent step up in peak from the treble crochet stitch.

Tall stitches have specific features, but they may be created in an identical way as the other primary stitches. So if you recognise a way to crochet double or treble crochet sew, the double treble stitch certainly requires a few more steps.

Yarn over three times
Whilst you're equipped to crochet a double treble crochet sew, step one is to yarn over the hook three times.

This makes sense while you keep in mind the other simple crochet stitches. As an example, while you make a double crochet stitch, you yarn over once.

While you make a treble crochet stitch, you yarn over two times. Because the double treble is the following tallest stitch, it is only herbal that you will yarn over three times.

Insert Hook

Insert the hook into the next stitch where the double treble crochet stitch is to be created.

That's exactly what you'd do to make a double crochet stitch or treble crochet, and you're just making the stitch bigger from step one with that extra "yarn over."

Yarn Over, Draw via loops on the hook.

Loop the yarn over the hook and draw via two of the loops in your hook—leaving four loops on the hook. Essentially you are repeating step 3 with fewer loops left at the hook every time.

Yarn Over, Draw Through

Keep Repeating Pattern

Continue Through the Last Two Loops

Whole Double Treble Crochet Sew

Repeat steps one to seven to create an entire row.

You will see that you may see notable stitch element with a stitch of this top

Guidelines for operating Double Treble Crochet Stitches

At the end of a row of treble crochet, you may chain five to turn.

You could use the double treble when crocheting in the remaining loop (the loop made whilst a sew executed in the again loop most effective) of a stitch numerous rows under.

The double treble is likewise often used whilst crocheting a front or lower back publish stitch around the point of another sew numerous rows under.

The double treble crochet stitch may be very flexible, and gaining knowledge of this approach will come up with getting admission to greater difficult styles.

In case you're developing a design, you could use this sew whilst a protracted chain is wanted.

You can also use it to make an undertaking a good way to crochet quick, or while you need larger breaks in the weave.

CONCLUSION

This book **CROCHET FOR BEGINNERS** *Learn step by step Crocheting with picture illustrations, Crochet patterns and stitches (Quick and easy guide);*

It isn't just a manual about crochet stiches for beginners, it's also contains advisory parts on how to go about crochetin and tools etc.

Take the details herein and sail in your interest for crochet stiches.

Mon. - tables
Wed -
Fri dessert
Thursday drinks
Sunday night
Tuesday dessert
saturday 11AM.